100 DAYS OF MONSTERS

BY STEFAN G. BUCHER

HOW BOOKS · CINCINNATI, OHIO
WWW.HOWDESIGN.COM

100 DAYS OF MONSTERS

Published by HOW Books, an imprint of F+W Publications, Inc.,
4700 East Galbraith Road, Cincinnati, Ohio 45236. (800) 289-0963.
For more fine books from F+W Publications, visit www.fwpublications.com

FIRST EDITION Hey! A first edition of "100 Days of Monsters"! That's exciting! You should store this copy in a cool, dark, and dry place to preserve it in mint condition. Then you can sell it 20 years down the line and use the money to pay your kid's tuition at MIT — That's the Monster Institute of Technology, by the way. (I intend to buy the school with my monster millions and rename it.) Hey! You should have me sign this one for you, so you can pay for tuition and living expenses! Right now you should buy a second copy of this book, so you can have a laugh until your investment matures.

12 11 10 09 08   5 4 3 2 1

Library of Congress Cataloging-in-Publication Data

Bucher, Stefan G.
    100 days of monsters / by Stefan G. Bucher. -- 1st ed.
        p. cm.
    Includes index.
    ISBN-13: 978-1-60061-091-2 (hardcover, with DVD : alk. paper)
    1. Monsters in art. 2. Drawing--Technique. I. Title. II. Title: One hundred days of monsters.
    NC825.M6B83 2008
    743'.87--dc22
                            2007042260

Please see page 219 for production credits.

Distributed in Canada by Fraser Direct
100 Armstrong Avenue
Georgetown, Ontario, Canada L7G 5S4
Tel: (905) 877- 4411

Distributed in the U.K. and Europe by David & Charles
Brunel House, Newton Abbot, Devon, TQ12 4PU, England
Tel: (+44) 1626-323200, Fax: (+44) 1626-323319
E-mail: postmaster@davidandcharles.co.uk

Distributed in Australia by Capricorn Link
P.O. Box 704, Windsor, NSW 2756 Australia
Tel: (02) 4577- 3555

WHO IS RESPONSIBLE FOR ALL THIS?

Stefan G. Bucher is a man possessed. When an idea pops into his head he can't stop until he somehow makes it real. Over the years this has led him to move from his native Germany to Southern California, where he got himself a degree from a killer art school. It pushed him to work as an art director at one of the world's best ad agencies in one of the world's wettest cities. It also got him fired from said agency less than a year later.

He then moved back to Los Angeles and became the man behind the 344 Design Empire. He has designed CD covers for just about every major record company and for a few minor ones, too. He has done work for Sting and Whitney Houston, and once rode in an elevator with the great Hunter S. Thompson three times in a row. (It's a long story.)

Now that everybody downloads their music on iTunes he has moved on to making books and art catalogs. He's good at it, too. British Design & Art Direction gave him a Yellow Pencil for "Most Outstanding Complete Book Design" for his design of the five-and-a-half pound *American Photography 17* annual, which—if you're not following the graphic design awards circuit—is a very impressive thing. In 2004 the Art Directors Club of New York declared him a Young Gun, which wasn't too shabby, either.

He wrote and designed the gratuitously ambitious book *All Access—The Making of 30 Extraordinary Graphic Designers* and spent two years writing and illustrating "ink & circumstance," a column on life, love and graphic design for *STEP inside design* magazine.

In his free time, Mr. Bucher enjoys...
Wait, strike that. Free time? Does not compute.
Mr. Bucher enjoys his work.

From: Ze Frank
To: Stefan G. Bucher
Date: Fri, 10 Aug 2007 14:43:59
Subject: Re: Monster Foreword

Dear Stefan—Of course I'm more than happy to write a foreword for your monster book. I regret not having participated in the project actively. Perhaps this is a chance for me to redeem myself; to react with a bit of reflection and whimsy to the wonderful monster that this project has become? I'm afraid, though, that you've given me far too much time to complete this assignment. I have quite a bit of free time on my hands and without a sense of urgency I'm afraid that I'll have to wait until the very last possible minute to get this done. Without anxiety I'm hopelessly lost.

Quick question: How much does one normally get paid for writing a foreword?

From: Ze Frank
Date: Sun, 12 Aug 2007 20:05:43

Nothing??? Why only ask for a thousand words? You should just write the words "The End" on a piece of paper, say it's your new book, and ask me to write a thousand page foreword.

From: Ze Frank
Date: Thu, 20 Sep 2007 11:32:05

In answer to your last e-mail: No, I have not started the foreword and don't have any clue as to what it will be about. Thank you, however, for your suggestions regarding *MY* FOREWORD.

You designers are all alike. You have to get your hands on everything. Remember when I called you a control freak? You corrected me and said, "I'm not a control freak, I'm a control enthusiast." That's exactly what a control freak would do— quibble about the verbiage. (Notice that you didn't take issue with the word "control"... Freak.)

From: Ze Frank
Date: Thu, 20 Sep 2007 13:01:27

Dear Stefan—I didn't mean control freak in the doesn't-play-well-with-others sort of way. What I mean is that you are details-oriented to a freakish degree. I'm sure Thi*S* w i l l m a k e you shu^{d}der. So wil\ *t* hi $. If I urge your readers to dog-ear the pages of your book you'll probably add perforation marks so that they do it at a perfect right angle.

When I first met you in San Diego you were showing a CD jacket that you'd recently completed. You kept zooming in. It was like a design fractal. At each magnification you pointed out something else that you'd manipulated and carefully considered, until these tiny little numbers in 4 pt. type were blown up so they covered the screen. You did this with each piece of work you presented.

It scared the crap out of me.

I am the opposite of a control freak, I live in the world of "close enough." If I were to build a house I would leave the trim unfinished, letting open seams linger for years. Watching you talk about your work made me wish I were more freakish about detail. You people have more fun. You go to picnics and bring bottle openers and little plastic stemmed glasses. Your handwriting is impeccable and the quilting on your toilet paper is chosen to ironically counter your bathroom wallpaper. You can zoom in on any part of your life and be proud.

This fractal pattern of detail is terrifying to me; an infinite number of things to tweak. It sometimes keeps me from starting new projects, and it is the reason you might never get your foreword.

P.S. Don't worry. I'm only half-not-kidding about not finishing the foreword.

From: Ze Frank
Date: Mon, 24 Sep 2007 10:41:23

Yes. I do remember that conversation. We were in Las Vegas eating dinner and you were wet and covered in confetti. Saying that I inspired you is quite unfair; I can't bear to be the inspiration for yet another project that won't make any money. All I said was that I wanted to watch you draw.

Let me explain why I said that. I'm sure that your perspective of that evening is very different than mine: Before we met for dinner, I was in the audience and you were on stage. At that point we were both dry and confetti free. The event had been billed as an "entertaining design game show." I'd been told that you would be competing against three other designers and overhead cameras would project your progress onto giant screens. I knew the tasks would be silly and impossible, but that didn't matter. I came to watch you draw. I wanted to see how those careful lines came out of your pen. And maybe, just a little, I wanted to see you fail.

Apparently the organizers didn't feel it would be entertaining enough to watch you try to design a logo, a business card and letterhead for a fictional company in five minutes. After all, that might be too ordinary for an audience of designers. We might say, "What's the big deal? We did that on Wednesday for a coffee company based in Cleveland, and they only gave us three minutes. And their slogan was 'Bean There, Done That.' And they had no budget."

No, this event needed to be bigger. Designer vs. Designer — Coliseum Style. But lions are too expensive, and in Vegas all the gladiators are in the cabaret union. So you were given crayons and glitter glue in lieu of your normal weaponry, and the moderator was hoisted up on a crane, armed with a water pistol and cans full of confetti: a *diabolus ex machina*. You fidgeted with pipe cleaners and tempera paint, and he shouted at you, and it rained wet confetti. It was an ancient and dark sort of comedy: Man vs. Insurmountable Obstacles. Designers vs. Circumstances Outside of Their Control.

It was a release valve for pressure that had been building up over many careers. The crayons were poorly trained interns, the confetti was a barrage of last-second spec changes, the water pistols were corporate style guides and the glitter glue was… well, I guess that was just glitter glue. Fact: Glitter glue is impervious to metaphor.

At the five minute bell (or was it a gong?) you held up your grotesque little objects, as disfigured and as wet as they were, and they were judged against the Initial Criteria. We laughed. "You failed! Ha! You couldn't win! Ha! Thank God that isn't me." We privately celebrated our own little victories against more boring and less moist forces outside of our control.

But I just wanted to watch you draw.

From: Ze Frank
Date: Mon, 24 Sep 2007 10:59:31

Yes, don't worry, you looked fine on stage. P.S. You have a huge, moon-shaped head.

From: Ze Frank
Date: Mon, 24 Sep 2007 23:15:42

Dear Moon Head — Just re-watched the videos hoping for some inspiration and noticed that you draw the titles upside down and inside out. Show-off.

I expected the drawings to be as controlled as those posters that you say take months to draw. Your monsters are instead pleasantly chaotic. I've loved ink spatters since I came across a page of Winsor McCay's *Dreams of the Rarebit Fiend*. The protagonist dreams that he is a cartoon at the mercy of his cartoonist. Panel by panel, McCay slowly destroys him, eventually reducing him to a spray of ink. You reverse the process, and build your little Frankensteins out of the wreckage. I especially like when you rotate the blot and search for some sign of life to latch onto.

I also like seeing all the lines that you draw, only to cover them up later with thick black marker. I can't tell if you are screwing up or feel more comfortable giving your monsters some kind of hidden form. It reminded me of the prodigious erotic nude sculpture Rodin made of Balzac, which he later covered with a cloak. (I'm glad you didn't draw erotic nude monsters.)

From: Ze Frank
Date: Tue, 27 Sep 2007 09:52:17

I see you have given me a hard deadline of one week. I take comfort in the fact that this is most likely not enough time to offer the job to someone else. I would be much more humiliated if I were replaced than if I failed to deliver. In the work I do online I rarely have hard deadlines. After something is released there are endless opportunities to edit, to erase, and to apologize for being late.

I apologize in advance.

From: Ze Frank
Date: Fri, 05 Oct 2007 12:07:36

Thank you. The images you sent are excellent. I do have one small issue. Considering the amount of anxiety that this foreword has caused me, I think my name should be a bit larger on the cover.

Your audience is really something. "Audience" is probably not the best word here. Is "contributors" better? But that might imply that you asked them to contribute, and from what you told me they started naming the monsters and telling stories without any prompting. Collaborators. Yes, your collaborators are really something. I'm glad that you embraced them, and I'm glad that they embraced you back. There's nothing more awkward than a one-sided hug. Except maybe writing "an one-sided hug."

All that online energy can be intimidating. Many designers talk about their fears of "losing control" to an online audience. They see a crowd assembling outside of their gates. ("What are they shouting?"

"I don't know, maybe they are hungry?" "OK, let them eat cake!") So they turn comments on, as some sort of a drainage pipe for all that energy, but the shouting doesn't stop. People spend hours writing about how no one should spend a single minute looking at this crap. And yet they stay.

Suddenly a little boy steps out of that crowd outside the gates and he has big brown eyes and is holding a little cap. You know what kind of boy I mean. And he says: "Excuse me. But we don't want to eat cake. In fact, we are sick and tired of eating all of this goddamn cake. We want to help BAKE the cake."

That's what you did, you let them help bake this cake. And I'm sure that it is much larger and more complex than you had imagined. Your monsters now have names, addresses, children and life histories. New monsters are being created from your downloadable blots and the tallest monster is getting taller. You started by drawing a monster a day and what you got was a living, breathing, growing context.

Did you lose a bit of control along the way? Maybe. But in the best conversations, relationships, handshakes, and ouija board sessions it is impossible to say who is in control. You listen and move together, generous with your time and with your praise. And when you're done you can lick the frosting off the spoon.

Ze

P.S. Forewords are supposed to add an outside perspective, additional context with which to appreciate a body of work. This book doesn't need a foreword from me. You've already included hundreds.

P.P.S. Do I still get a free book?

Ze Frank is a digital age storyteller and consultant. He rose to Internet fame in 2001 with his viral video "How to Dance Properly," and has been making online comedy and web toys ever since. *The Show With Ze Frank* drew thousands of viewers daily during its recent year-long run. You can find him online at zefrank.com

How are you? We're already a couple of pages into the book, so I hope it's not too late to say *hello*.

It's your pal Stefan here, and if you're not familiar with the Daily Monsters I should explain—about the creatures, about the website, and about this book. Let's call it

MONSTERS 101.

Just a few months ago, I spent 100 days filming myself drawing 100 monsters based on random ink blots. I put them on my website, dailymonster.com. To my total surprise over 150,000 people from all over the world came to visit and downloaded the monsters over half a million times. Better yet, hundreds of people got in touch with their inner author and posted strange, funny and amazing stories about each creature. This book collects all 100 Daily Monsters along with over 400 stories from the website. Better yet, there's a DVD in the back of the book that has all 100 monster videos, a PDF with all the stories in the book, and an extra 200 stories that simply didn't fit on these pages.

How did all this come about?

The very first monster came to visit me in the first week of May, back in 2006. It was a sunny afternoon. I was driving on the 10 East freeway here in L.A. Just as I was curving onto the 110 freeway to go home to Pasadena, I saw an inky black monster wind itself around my right arm. (I don't drink or do drugs, and this is one of the reasons why. I see things like that all the time. I don't need the help.) So there I was, driving along with a monster

curled around my arm. It seemed like a friendly beast and I thought *I should draw you, shouldn't I?*

Over the weeks that followed I drew all kinds of creatures. They came to me quickly and in all shapes and sizes. I gave each of them a name and collected them in a book.

This is not that book. That book was called *Upstairs Neighbors*. I showed it to publishers, and a few of them actually wanted to put it out. Those were exciting days.

Then came the waiting. Publishers can take a long, long time to make up their minds. Some told me *no* after a few weeks, others took six months. Some of them are still getting ready to say *yes* today. In the beginning I was pretty mad about it. Why didn't they welcome my monsters with open arms? Now I'm glad that they didn't say *yes* right away, because of what happened next.

I got impatient. I don't like waiting for things to happen. I like *doing* stuff. I decided to make a drawing a day to keep myself occupied. My plan was to draw things on my desk, things I'd see on my porch or in town: pens, flowers, hummingbirds, girls. I wanted to call it the Daily Doodle. As it turned out, there are about ten sites featuring a Daily Doodle already. What else could I draw daily? Hm. Hm. Hmmm... I googled "Daily Monster" and found nothing but a wide open space calling out to me. And so, half by chance, the Daily Monsters were born.

A little past 7:00 P.M. on November 18, I set up my little digital camera, flipped it to movie mode and filmed Daily Monster 01. I put a few drops of black sumi ink on a sheet of bond paper and blew them into a shape.

I turned the sheet a few times to see what I had, and there it was—a monster bird looking back at me. All I had to do was put some lines around it to make it visible to everybody else.

When I was done, I made a simple opening credit for the clip. I wrote it upside down and backwards, because I thought it would be more interesting that way. Writing upside down and backwards is actually not that difficult. Once you figure out the *N* and the *S* it's easy. (Mind you, the *4* can be tricky, too, but you shouldn't let that stop you.)

After that was done, I squished the whole little movie into one minute, because watching somebody draw five times faster than normal is at least five times more fun. The last stop was putting the monster online so my friends could see it. That's who I thought would watch these clips. I mean… who else would care? In fact, I didn't even *tell* my friends about the monsters at first. Honestly, I was worried that I'd drop the ball on doing a monster a day or that the whole thing would somehow be boring to watch.

Boy, did I have it all wrong. After the first week (and a link from Russell Davies) I noticed that I had over 200 visitors a day. In week two my friends at *SpeakUp* posted a story about the project, and suddenly I had 1,000 visitors a day. Then Ze unleashed his disciples on me and everything went crazy.

It was exciting to have so many visitors, but that wasn't the best part. What *really* blew my mind was that people started giving the monsters names. They told me what music the monsters liked, where they worked, what they did for fun. I'd post a monster at midnight, and by morning there'd be stories waiting from all around the world—Australia, Japan, Europe, South America, Canada, and from all over the U.S. For 100 days the sun never set on the monsters.

Over time the monsters got more involved. I started drawing them upside down, just to see if I could. I added small animations at the end—simple stop motion tricks that turned into more elaborate sequences as I taught myself a cheap little animation program called Anime Studio. All through this time the stories got weirder, and greater, and funnier! The writers started talking to each other, giving praise and collaborating on stories, egging each other on. Somehow the Daily Monsters had become a seed crystal for a brilliant community of creative people.

There were times when I'd get exhausted—some of the animations took eight, nine, ten hours at the end of my regular work day—but seeing everybody's stories always gave me the energy I needed. The stories and the excellent people behind them are the reason you're now holding this book. I wanted to create a time capsule of this odd little lark that developed a life of its own.

I didn't plan any of this, but I'm so glad it happened. I've been drawing since I could hold a pencil, and I've always been happy when I got another drawing done. But after all these years, these monsters are the first drawings that are fun *while* I'm drawing them.

I hope you have fun with them, too.

So that's the story of how the monsters came to be. "But wait!" you might say, "Why are there 100 monsters? Why not 50? Or 344? Or 1,000? Or one for every day of the year?" These are valid questions, but I'm not the man with the answers. I'm just the guy that allows the monsters entry into our world by means of ink. Why 100 monsters? I decided to ask a few of the most prolific authors in the Daily Monster universe. Here are their answers.

WHY 100 MONSTERS?

Monsters, aliens—whatever. These creatures clearly aren't from Earth. It is a little-known fact that Mr. 344 came into possession of a rare unstable element called Stommerinium. The details of how he obtained and stored the element are unknown, but what it does is well-known. Mr. 344 sprinkles some of the powder into his inkwell and

the combination of Stommerinium and ink creates a portal to the mirrors the monsters gaze into.

The ink morphs into the shape of a monster that happens to be looking in a mirror, and Mr. 344 fills out the rest. The reason there are only 100 is that there is no Stommerinium left (in Mr. 344's stash at least). That is why other people are drawing monsters now.

Alexander Pollard (Plymouth, Massachusetts)
35 posts in 100 days

A manila envelope's flap gently seals the documents within. Thick, black marker scrolls lettering upon the front. A one-word name, Leyland[1], above "Cardinal[2] Way" blots the paper. Countless hours of research lie inside. A worthy investment of time and energy.

Commissioned study by a benefactor known, curiously, as Roman C.[3] Hecto.[4]

Each sheet holding invaluable details about each subject. Illustrations and words to accompany that which the world must know. Unique creatures possessing unique qualities. Mr. Bucher had discovered them all. A group connected by a numerical prophecy of hope and prosperity. The cover page inscribed with, simply: "Centinals."[5]

First, there are 100 words. No more, no less.

[1] **Leyland:** The number 100 is the 6th number of the form xy + yx, where x and y are natural numbers; thus making it a Leyland number.

[2] **Cardinal:** the generalized form of a number to denote a set. There are 100 in the set. (An "ordinal" would be 100th)

[3] **Roman C.:** The Roman Numeral for 100 is C.

[4] **Hecto:** The Greek prefix for 100 (hectometer, hectogon).

[5] **Centi(nals):** The Latin prefix for 100 (centimeter, centipede).

Terry Tolleson (Austin, Texas)
75 posts in 100 days

The day it began was a day like any other. Nothing special, just your average day. No sign from above, no thunder flashes or blinding light. Nothing to indicate that this was going to be the day that Stefan G. Bucher would be hit by genius.

The idea flashed into his head in an instant. I'll draw a different monster every day. And upload the whole thing to the web. The name followed seamlessly. I'll call it Daily Monster. Everything so effortless, so perfect.

And then it stalled. How long should this run for? How many daily monsters should there be?

Slowly the answers came. Stefan G. Bucher's first thought was 99. But this seemed unfulfilling, incomplete, disappointing in the way a cheeseburger is when you've been shortchanged on the Swiss.

His second thought was 101. But that seemed just, well, just a touch too much, like taking a chocolate cream donut and covering it in honey.

And then the genius returned.
There would be 100 monsters. It fit perfectly:

More than 99, but less than 101.

A little more Swiss, a lot less honey.

Yes, thought Stefan G. Bucher, smiling a grin just the right side of insane. There would be 100 Daily Monsters. No more. No less.

Simon Darwell-Taylor (London, England)
18 posts in 100 days

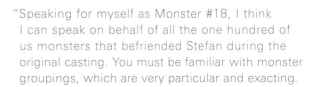

"Speaking for myself as Monster #18, I think I can speak on behalf of all the one hundred of us monsters that befriended Stefan during the original casting. You must be familiar with monster groupings, which are very particular and exacting.

If he drew us in a posse of 32, or 98, or 106, it would not a proper Torment make.

The crows, they have their Murders and bacteria, their Cultures and Colonies. Fish with their Schools and geese with their Gaggles. Crikey, even the humans have their Litters… or wait, is that dogs—erm, cats… pigs!? Anyway… monsters have their Torments and Stefan, being the wise human with very vulnerable parts, listens to reason and respects the order and science of things.

And also, because drawing a googol of us (at least in one go) would leave our dear Mister Bucher precious little time to do naught else! Well, add to that the fact that he's the only one around here with a straw. We can never find a decent straw to blow each other with. Our Stefan is the one who breathes life into us after all."

Victoria Koldewyn (Eugene, Oregon)
82 posts in 100 days

Stefan Bucher blew some ink onto the page,
raised a Sharpie up on high, and said,
"O bless this inky blot that it mayest move my
patrons to writeth some stories." And writeth
they did, feasting on new monsters daily.
The end, it seemed, was nowhere in sight.
But Bucher, creator of monsters daily,
upon sight of number 60, spake, saying,

"I shalt draw to one hundred, no more, no less.

One hundred shall be the number,
and the number shall be one hundred.
One hundred and one shalt I not draw,
neither shalt I draw ninety nine, excepting
that I then proceed to one hundred.
One hundred and two is right out. Once
the number one hundred is reached,
the daily monsters will beist no more
(weekly monsters excepting). So it has
been spoken, so it shall be done."

Sayeth Stefan Bucher,
creator of the monsters daily.

Sam Berkes (Peoria Heights, Illinois)
102 posts in 100 days

Stefan befriends Crazy Cat Lady, whose
one hundred cats steal his heart. He has
no previous affinity for any previous cat,
but Crazy Cat Lady and her feline entourage
rouse him. He is inspired.

The first inspiration comes from a pattern of kitty litter stuck to the sole of his foot.

He shifts this to ink and monster one is born.
Yearning to repay the cats for his newfound
inspiration, he decides upon a monster for each.
He draws for one hundred days. The last
monster is drawn and he presents them to
the cats. They are pleased. He is fulfilled.
He dreams good things for the cats and the
monsters, and is honored when they decide
to publish. The cats unite and write stories
for each monster. They bind the book of stories
and beasts and give it to Stefan.
A single tear forms. He is complete.

Brooke Nelson (Peoria Heights, Illinois)
12 posts in 100 days

Hunnert felt bloated. The nice humanoid at the corner shop ("Get the latest issue of Monster Weekly here! Five tasty Snogostents for a dollar! Ten packets of MonsterRamen for a dollar!") was entirely to blame.

"Hey," he'd whispered to Hunnert one day almost three and a half months ago, "there's a new promotion going on." Hunnert was a sucker for promotions. "Oh?" he asked casually, only inside, he was so gum-didly-umptiously anxious to hear that he could hardly wait. "What is it?"

The humanoid pushed his glasses up on his nose. Hunnert's mother had said never to trust a humanoid wearing glasses, but Hunnert ignored her. "You'll get a terrific prize if you can just eat 101 monsters in a row." Hunnert loved prizes. "What kind of prize?"

The man leaned forward. "Big secret."

He rubbed his hand over his head, and Hunnert noticed he had no hair. "Never trust a bald humanoid," Hunnert's mother echoed in his ear. Hunnert ignored it and purchased his first monster. It was a blobbly squirmy flippity thing, and Hunnert had to wrestle it in order to eat it. It tasted of black licorice. Hunnert loved licorice. "Do they all taste this way?"

The humanoid smiled. He had a lot of evenly spaced, square teeth. "Some of them are laced with raspberry," he said, and Hunnert went home and looked up raspberries in the dictionary.

That was such a long time ago. The humanoid hadn't told him that monsters don't digest. They just sit there, rumbling about in your belly, until you hear them in your head, practically, scrambling with all of their funky little life stories.

Today Hunnert ate monster 100, right there in front of the humanoid. The humanoid smiled. Then Hunnert burped, a huge, flame-throwing belch that echoed through the store. It scorched everything, and the humanoid blinked. "Well," he said, "I guess you've reached your limit. You were so close!"

"But...but..." spluttered Hunnert. "Then I don't get anything?" "Oh, no, you get something very special," said the humanoid, and he smiled with all of his teeth and passed Hunnert a hard flat something. "What is this?" Hunnert turned the thing over in his claws. Loose bits, like leaves from the squashysquarebobpsy plant in Hunnert's mother's garden, fluttered. "What do I do with it?"

"It's a book," said the humanoid, "You read it." "Oh," said Hunnert, and, feeling a bit of indigestion, he ate the thing. It was just one too much. Hunnert exploded, raining book pages and monsters all over the universe.

Yi Shun Lai (Chicago, Illinois)
32 posts in 100 days

01

Drawing:
Saturday, 18 Nov 2006, 07:30 P.M.
Drawing posted:
Sunday, 19 Nov 2006, 01:04 A.M.

Loving it! It's kinda like Toucan Sam on crack.

By Megan Koehler | November 19, 2006 at 07:53 P.M.

Short little feet
had Monster One
and a fat long nose
that liked to run

But the desire of
the beast of wonder
was to have a clear nose
and feet like a runner

So advice was asked
and everyone said
that shoes were needed
with lots of tread

By cygnus | February 09, 2007 at 11:15 P.M.

Bird of prey? Hardly!

Toucan Stu is a bird of party. Seen from time to time
at the hottest dance clubs NYC has to offer,
Toucan Stu really brings the funk. He's been offered
good money to promote new clubs but as we all know,
Toucan Stu doesn't advertise.

By Sam Berkes | February 25, 2007 at 07:18 A.M.

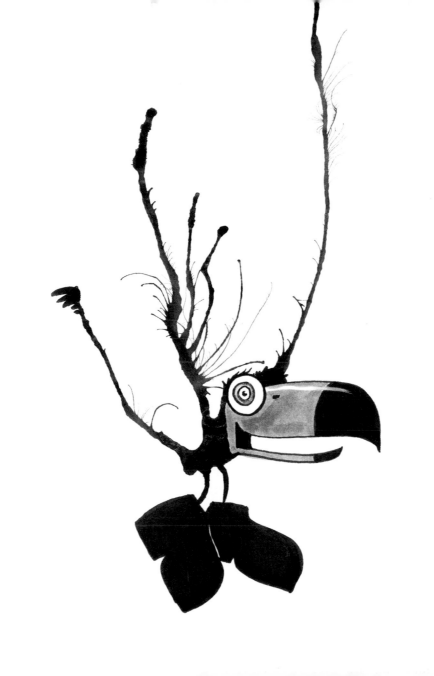

02

Drawing:
Sunday, 19 Nov 2006, 04:45 P.M.
Drawing posted:
Sunday, 19 Nov 2006, 09:24 P.M.

This is Licorice the Hutt,
brother of Pizza the Hutt.
Some people like him;
some can't stand him at all.
Story of his life.

Licorice was slated to appear
in *Spaceballs* beside his bro Pizza
but failed to make the cut.
I suppose he left a bad taste
in Mel's mouth.

By Sam Berkes | February 25, 2007 at 07:34 A.M.

03

It began with a pony,
evolved into a soaring eagle,
and will soon be going Gastropoda.

Embracing the negative "Snail Mail" connotation, the USPS hopes to cash in on the moniker by trademarking the name.

The new mascot, Hes Cargot, is seen here. Cute little fellow, isn't he?

By Sam Berkes | March 06, 2007 at 06:42 P.M.

Drawing:
Tuesday, 21 Nov 2006, 02:30 A.M.
Drawing posted:
Tuesday, 21 Nov 2006, 10:48 A.M.

Oh Man. Today's monster is my fave.

Crazed dog.
That must be
how you feel like
on the inside...

Happy Thanksgiving.

By Susan Lee | November 22, 2006 at 03:06 P.M.

Yes... but like your monster-critter,
you manage to have one big eye open,
never missing a *thing!*

By Amanda Wray | November 22, 2006 at 07:04 P.M.

Drawing:
Tuesday, 21 Nov 2006, 08:45 P.M.
Drawing posted:
Wednesday, 22 Nov 2006, 02:31 A.M.

Do you understand, sir?
The fight is close at hand, sir.

Birds with teeth bite bugs in flight.
This bug's flight is fraught with plight.
This bug's fright of bite is right,
As this bird's bite displays such plight.

But birds and bugs still meet and fight.
Bugs and birds with feet soon might,
Meet and greet and fight 'til plight.

By Sam Berkes | March 05, 2007 at 03:00 P.M.

Drawing:
Tuesday, 21 Nov 2006, 10:10 P.M.
Drawing posted:
Wednesday, 22 Nov 2006, 08:55 P.M.

06

Drawing:
Tuesday, 21 Nov 2006, 10:30 P.M.
Drawing posted:
Thursday, 23 Nov 2006, 09:36 P.M.

Happy Thanksgiving!
I hope you had a lovely, mellow day
of sharing good food
with good friends and family.
I did.

In fact, I don't think I've worried
about kerning once today.
But I did remember to post
a new monster for you.

It's a turkey leftover sandwich made of ink.

Enjoy and know that 344 LOVES YOU.

By Stefan G. Bucher | November 23, 2006 at 09:36 P.M.

Some of you have asked me
how I make the monsters:

How do you do these "airbrushes"?
What do you call this technique?
How do you make the opening credits look
like you're writing upside down and in reverse?

The technique is called "blown ink."
You just take a straw and blow on a drop of ink.
It's that simple.

As for the opening credits, there is no trick:
I write them upside down and in reverse.
Why? Because I'm a show-off.

By Stefan G. Bucher | November 27, 2006 at 12:07 P.M.

Drawing:
time not recorded
Drawing posted:
Saturday, 25 Nov 2006, 12:36 A.M.

Stanus Alsterprix.

From the wealthy Gruvenorenstein shipping family.
He was a bit more mutated than the rest of his family
and was always an outcast. He decided he wanted
to live with no ties to his family or others, so he changed
his last name and decided to drive a truck for a living.

He uses the feet to stand on the seat, the long
appendage goes to the steering wheel,
the forked appendage works the pedals and
the rear appendage is to switch gears.

He has been known to pick up hitchhikers,
although many refuse rides. He is a quiet man
content with driving his deliveries back and forth.

Ironically, he works for his family company.
He knows this, but they don't.
Since he changed his name
they will never find out.

By Alex Pollard | December 18, 2006 at 07:58 A.M.

Drawing:
Wednesday, 22 Nov 2006, 01:00 A.M.
Drawing posted:
Sunday, 26 Nov 2006, 12:01 A.M.

09

Drawing:
Monday, 27 Nov 2006, 04:45 P.M.
Drawing posted:
Monday, 27 Nov 2006, 05:09 P.M.

Wow! Up until you drew the tail
I thought this monster
was facing the other way.

By Gareth Townsend | November 28, 2006 at 03:46 A.M.

Ah yes! I see what you mean, Gareth!
Boy... that way 'round he'd have been VERY sinister!

By Stefan G. Bucher | November 28, 2006 at 04:49 A.M.

Katherine also had this monster pegged
the other way around, kind of strutting,
with its arms stretched out.
We love guessing which way it turns out.

By Joerg Metzner | November 28, 2006 at 05:47 A.M.

10

What do you do with the monsters
when you've finished them?

By Jen Rodis | November 28, 2006 at 10:49 A.M.

Hi Jen. When I'm done with each monster,
I put the date and time on it, then I put it
in an acid-free archival storage box along with
all my other drawings. They may end up
in a book or on a wall someday, or they may
just stay in the box forever. Hard to say
at this point. Their main function is as raw
material for these film clips.

By Stefan G. Bucher | November 28, 2006 at 12:34 P.M.

Stefan, this is the best ever.
Living in the land of the mozzies,
I SO relate!

By Catherine Morley | November 29, 2006 at 02:05 A.M.

Drawing:
Tuesday, 28 Nov 2006, 04:45 A.M.
Drawing posted:
Tuesday, 28 Nov 2006, 05:59 A.M.

11

Drawing:
Tuesday, 28 Nov 2006, 10:45 A.M.
Drawing posted:
Wednesday, 29 Nov 2006, 12:32 A.M.

Can I propose Albert as being a good name?

By Simon Darwell-Taylor | November 29, 2006 at 01:15 A.M.

For you, I will give you the name
I have been saving
for my first-born child,
whether it was a boy or girl.

Drum roll please. The name is...
CLEMENTINE.

By Susan Lee | November 29, 2006 at 04:07 A.M.

Horris the Humdrumbler is cautious
Do you know why?

By Sam Berkes | November 29, 2006 at 06:19 A.M.

This thing is definitely a Quirkifonaptor,
a species known for its outlandish talents
in belly blooping and napkin nobbing.

By Megan Koehler | November 29, 2006 at 10:12 P.M.

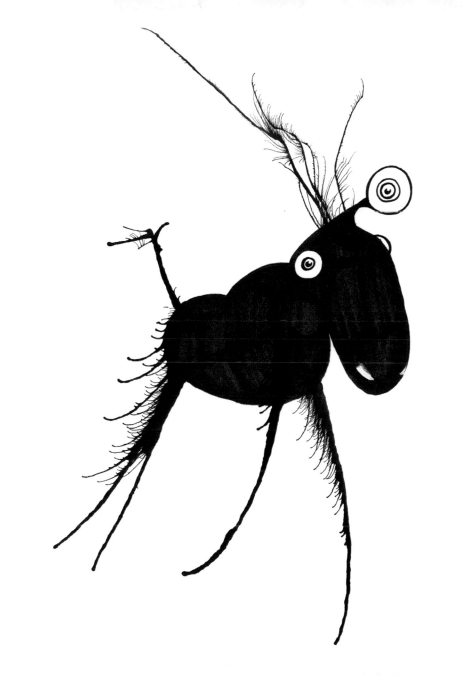

He is a floss salesman.

And judging from his pearly white tusks,
he samples the goods before selling them.

By Sam Berkes | November 30, 2006 at 07:26 A.M.

I swear he is working in that dimly lit back room
in our cartography department
here at Rand McNally.

By Joerg Metzner | November 30, 2006 at 09:02 A.M.

This is most certainly a portrait of the guy
who comes to fix our poorly built college home.
He always has roots in his mouth from using
special machinery to cut the roots out of our old
broken drainage pipes. Healthy diet for this guy,
but not the optimal dinner guest.

By Kyle Fletcher | November 30, 2006 at 12:10 P.M.

Drawing:
Wednesday, 29 Nov 2006, 11:45 P.M.
Drawing posted:
Thursday, 30 Nov 2006, 06:48 A.M.

13

Drawing:
Thursday, 30 Nov 2006, 06:05 P.M.
Drawing posted:
Friday, 01 Dec 2006, 12:22 A.M.

Brooke's Monster 13 Playlist:

1. "On My Way Home" — Three
2. "Where's Max" — 3
3. "Over and Over" — Three Days Grace
4. "Darwin" — Third Eye Blind
5. "The Sun Is Shining" — Third Day

By Brooke Nelson | December 01, 2006 at 07:04 A.M.

Adding to Brooke's list:
"Joy to the World" by Three Dog Night.

By Sam Berkes | December 01, 2006 at 07:15 P.M.

I would've also accepted "Eli's Coming" by Three Dog Night,
but I like the bullfrog angle. We might add "1-2-3"
by the Miami Sound Machine, or the obscure
but lovely "3:00 A.M. Blues" by the Dick Hyman Group
featuring Howard Alden. Brooke Nelson really set us
on the right path here. Thank you, Brooke!

By Stefan G. Bucher | December 01, 2006 at 08:07 P.M.

14

Alfred E. Neuman meets the Cyclops

Sort of like *Abbott and Costello Meet the Wolfman,*
with its lineup of Universal monsters, all in the one movie.

The *MAD* magazine mascot takes a hiatus from
the cover of the magazine to a tropical and
mysteriously deserted island and encounters
the REAL versions of Don Martin's cartoons…
with cameos by assorted characters
from Merrie Melodies and varied Hanna-Barbera cartoons.

Also starring Tom Waits
(with a soundtrack by him)
and Sandra Bernhard.

By Pete Pringle | December 14, 2006 at 09:17 P.M.

Drawing:
Thursday, 30 Nov 2006, 06:15 P.M.
Drawing posted:
Saturday, 02 Dec 2006, 01:05 A.M.

0015 is the size of an average dog, near the upper part of your shin, not including the eyes.

0015 evolved this way in a dark environment that required multiple eyes to see and absorb as much light as possible. A beak to eat nutlike foods dropped from trees in the ankle-high water terrain.

The tail is for balance and the shoes are to help 0015 cope with its unfortunate disorder of weak-soled feet.

The heels are 0015's personal taste.

By Danielle Ngo | December 03, 2006 at 04:50 P.M.

Drawing:
Thursday, 30 Nov 2006, 06:25 P.M.
Drawing posted:
Sunday, 03 Dec 2006, 12:41 A.M.

This is one of my favorite monsters so far,

16 SUCH A LOVELY GRIN!

I'm dedicating "Drive My Car" and "Lady Madonna" to this guy.

By **Simon Zirkunow** | December 04, 2006 at 04:16 A.M.

Drawing:
Thursday, 30 Nov 2006, 06:35 P.M.
Drawing posted:
Sunday, 03 Dec 2006, 11:35 P.M.

17

He's mad because Don King is his hair stylist.
That's proposteriffical.

By **Sam Berkes** | December 05, 2006 at 07:53 A.M.

Drawing:
Thursday, 30 Nov 2006, 06:45 P.M.
Drawing posted:
Tuesday, 05 Dec 2006, 01:31 A.M.

Perhaps he just needs
a good cup of joe
and a great big hug.
And maybe a comb.

By **Catherine Morley** | December 05, 2006 at 09:08 A.M.

He's mad because his cousin Beaker
got all the fame and fortune on *The Muppet Show.*

By **Amber Himes** | December 05, 2006 at 12:12 P.M.

He's mad because the lack of sleep from last night
made his eyes all kooky and today is his
most important eye-modeling shoot.

By **Danielle Ngo** | December 05, 2006 at 06:13 P.M.

18

His name is Crustaceous Phil. He lives in the basement apartment of a five-story walk-up, not far from Times Square. He doesn't mind the dangers of living in a dark basement with poor ventilation and no light. His favorite TV show is *Futurama*.

By Sam Berkes | December 06, 2006 at 07:42 A.M.

Drawing:
Thursday, 30 Nov 2006, 06:55 P.M.
Drawing posted:
Wednesday, 06 Dec 2006, 01:36 A.M.

Good Lord! That's no monster! That's my Uncle Jaques!

He's sixty-one, lives in northern Minnesota, has a house painting business, chain smokes and drinks Old Milwaukee. I have no idea what his favorite TV show is, but he would probably enjoy *Trick My Truck* on CMT. Not sure why he's wearing that silly robe, though. Maybe his coveralls are in the dryer.

By Emily H. Murphy | December 06, 2006 at 11:03 A.M.

I'm not sure he's wearing a robe, it looks more like a trench coat... one that flashers wear. Could he be a flasher??? Maybe he's getting ready to streak through the streets and is looking up to make sure that it won't rain.

Is he wearing platforms?

By Diane Witman | December 08, 2006 at 08:21 A.M.

19

Well I think it's quite obvious:

This is Fada Cripness, the dark,
lesser-known twin brother of Santa.

According to Laplandish folklore, when the twins were born,
Santa, despite being 186 seconds younger than Fada,
quickly established himself as the favorite to become heir
to the family heirlooms of cape and sack and supersonic sleigh.

With Santa getting all the attention from his parents and
the elves as they taught him the family business,
Fada found himself alone with his anger. It was after the incident
with the cemented-in chimney that Fada was banished
to the reindeer stables where he learnt the dark skills. Which
he put to devastating effects in 1793. Skillfully hushed up
by Rudolph, the legend of Father Christmas survived,
but to prevent it ever happening again Fada was sealed
into the Caves of Waddau. That is where he remained
until this year when, rumor has it, a careless pot-holer
accidentally facilitated his escape.

Unfortunately, this year will not be
a very merry Christmas, for any of us.

By Simon Darwell-Taylor | December 07, 2006 at 01:47 A.M.

Drawing:
Wednesday, 06 Dec 2006, 01:00 P.M.
Drawing posted:
Thursday, 07 Dec 2006, 01:06 A.M.

20

Drawing:
Wednesday, 06 Dec 2006, 01:15 P.M.
Drawing posted:
Friday, 08 Dec 2006, 01:34 A.M.

Jogo YangLang never liked dogs very much, probably because she spent her first seven years lodged inside a Great Dane's ear. She'd never enjoyed it, not even at the beginning when he was a puppy, which was why on 29 October 1973 at precisely 3:17 A.M. she sneaked out of the kennel hidden under the shell of a dead tick. She traveled and found work where she could; eventually she found herself cold and wet in Hamburg; the year was 1988.

Since then her time spent lap dancing has left her with a dodgy knee and a taste for the finer things in life. If you want to be her sugar daddy **you can find her most nights in the VIP lounge of the Hippity-Hoppity Club.**

By Simon Darwell-Taylor
December 08, 2006 at 04:12 A.M.

Seldom seen in the wild, the Roller-toe Snipe-tongue is graceful and elegant. Originating in Xalapa, the capital city of Veracruz, Mexico, the Snipe-tongue has adapted to extreme desert conditions. Vestigial legs hidden beneath a thick layer of abdominal tissue help it to traverse through deep sand and gravel when its rollers get stuck.

This particular individual, Tulipán Feo, is thought to be related to the mystical Florecita. Florecita are believed in Spanish folklore to be the most beautiful women in the world. From the looks of it, Tulipán Feo, and others like her, are very distant relatives.

Once thought to have kept ties to the Xalapa region for personal reasons, the Snipe-tongue have been seen in certain parts of the United States. In sister city Covina, California, for example, rare sightings of Roller-toe Snipe-tongues have been reported.

Most likely they migrated to the United States via transport of jalapeño peppers. It has been noted that they lack pain receptors in their long proboscis-like tongues when it comes to capsaicin, and so have developed a taste for the peppers over time.

By Sam Berkes | December 08, 2006 at 07:28 A.M.

Drawing:
Thursday, 07 Dec 2006, 12:55 A.M.
Drawing posted:
Saturday, 09 Dec 2006, 02:00 A.M.

What a wonderful surprise. I thought everyone had forgotten about Waldo "The Worm" Gritti (who got his name because his head was always in a book). And at No.21! He would have so loved that. And not just because of his love of numbers.

As you might recall Waldo was the bookkeeper of Tono "Twinkle Toes" Trovelli (who got his name because of his seven very small feet).

From time to time, Twinkle Toes Trovelli would take Waldo to see Lassi Laski, yes THE Lassi Laski (who got her name from her parents). Seeing them in the front row centre, she knew she had to dance The Dance of the Thirteen Tentacles, even though it filled her with dread.

After the show, they would go backstage where Twinkle Toes would maul Lassi, while Waldo was forced to watch.

One night backstage, after the twenty-first time they'd seen Lassi dance, Waldo made his fatal mistake;

unable to take Lassi's humiliation he hit Twinkle Toes really, really hard on his arm with a first edition of *Debit and Loss 2.0*.

What a horrid mistake to make. As of course this led to such acts I cannot bring myself to write about.

Waldo, you fool. She had never even noticed you.

By Simon Darwell-Taylor | December 09, 2006 at 04:48 A.M.

Huffenstuffenpuffen hasn't worked for a long time now.
At one time, he'd been famous. Always working. Never stopping.
In the '60s he appeared on most of the Rolling Stones' hits.
In the '70s it was the complete catalogue of the Jackson Five.
In the '80s if it wasn't Wham! it was Duran Duran. Ask him
and he would say his proudest moment was probably being
on Imagination's *Body Talk* white label EP.

But all that is behind him now. Now he sits in the corner
of The Kings Arms, Carnaby Street, London, where every night
around closing time he can be heard telling anyone and
everyone about his glory days, hidden in the grooves of LPs
wrestling with giant needles armed with nothing more
than a handful of fluff.

By Simon Darwell-Taylor | December 10, 2006 at 04:12 A.M.

Drawing:
Thursday, 07 Dec 2006, 01:16 A.M.
Drawing posted:
Sunday, 10 Dec 2006, 01:42 A.M.

This is Stevie Slugworth.
It's his first day at his new job,
and he's very excited about that.

He's been employed by a famous department store, and his job is to stand in the cosmetics department and point to the escalators when tourists ask.

He was recommended for the job
by his second cousin once removed.

By Amanda Doria | December 10, 2006 at 06:28 P.M.

Emlyn, age 4: She was going to the lake. She swimmed at the lake.
Then she went to the city and slept in a bed. Then she woke up
and gave everyone she knowed flowers. That's it!

By Sarah Schopp | February 10, 2007 at 02:18 P.M.

23

Drawing:
Thursday, 07 Dec 2006, 01:30 A.M.
Drawing posted:
Monday, 11 Dec 2006, 12:31 A.M.

When Dr. Hucklestein first went to college it was with a very different heart than the one he left with. It had started off as just student high jinks. No one can remember who had suggested it, but someone had: "Hey, I know, let's get Hunchback Hucky drunk and swap his heart with Brutus's." Brutus was the campus guard dog.

Such are the minds of young medical students, that before you knew it pints of gin were being poured and the bedroom with the coats in it was being sterilized. Obviously the next morning it didn't seem so funny to anyone, but what could they do?

Much later while working with his good friend and old dorm mate Dr. Frankenstein, Dr. Hucklestein became interested in the use of electricity as a means of bringing life to inanimate objects. In the beginning they worked closely together on ways in which to harness the power of storms. But all that changed one night when, after a hard day in the lab, they got very drunk in the local tavern.

The next morning, Dr. Hucklestein woke with the mother of all hangovers. At first he thought that was why he wobbled.

But weeks later—his hangover a distant shudder of regret—he was still hobbling. And then there was that scar that went completely around the top of his leg, which he was sure hadn't been there before. Plus now he needed a size six shoe on his left foot when in the past both feet had fitted snugly into a size eight. When he asked Dr. Frankenstein about that night, Dr. Frankenstein, refusing to hold his gaze, said he knew nothing.

In the coming weeks, tensions continued to build until it was impossible for either doctor to be in the same lab as one another, no matter how dark it was. It had a devastating effect on Dr. Hucklestein, who finally left medical research altogether to set up a very successful dog food emporium.

By Simon Darwell-Taylor | December 11, 2006 at 01:29 A.M.

Ever since Dr. Hucklestein's falling out with good ole Dr. Frankenstein he hasn't been able to get "The Scientist" by Coldplay out of his (rather large) head.

By Laura Barry | December 11, 2006 at 07:02 A.M.

24

the best ballet dancer the world had ever seen.

Drawing:
Tuesday, 12 Dec 2006, 01:15 A.M.
Drawing posted:
Tuesday, 12 Dec 2006, 04:30 A.M.

Though hands are missing
Zula knows to keep kicking
The show must go on

By Sam Berkes
December 12, 2006 at 08:22 A.M.

This is, of course, *the* Lassi Laski, Waldo Gritti's (Monster 21) unrequited love interest. Possibly one of the most evil choreographers ever born. She was born to Austrian nobility and schooled by private tutors in an impossibly beautiful castle. Her early years had been perfect, some say too perfect. At four she was given a 137-piece Wedgwood tea set. At five, a pony. At eight she was taken to her first ballet, The Nutcracker Suite, and she became hooked. From that day onwards she knew what she wanted to become, a ballet dancer, a great ballet dancer,

Count Laski, her father, pulled some strings, applied a little political pressure and killed Count Preud in a duel to ensure that she got a place at the Salzburg International Ballet Academy.

Lassi worked hard, harder than anyone there, harder than anyone had ever worked at the Academy, but unfortunately she had zero talent. Eventually Count Laski's dueling could protect her no longer and she was asked to leave. Sinking in depression, Lassi started to hang out with a bad crowd, one of whom was a weird vegetarian painter called Adolf. And it was that chance encounter that changed history, for as we know Lassi several years later she became the official choreographer for the Nazi party and inventor of the Storm Trooper Goose Step March.

By Simon Darwell-Taylor | December 12, 2006 at 05:10 A.M.

Caroline always wanted a pony, and being that it was near Christmas she thought maybe her time had come. She ignored the fact that her parents said they couldn't afford a horse, the upkeep and the riding lessons. She didn't understand why they kept talking about getting her a turtle — a turtle is nothing like a horse! You can't ride a turtle, brush its hair or feed it apples!

It came to a head on December 12th. During dinner Caroline kept talking about names for the horse and what colors she wanted him (she wanted a boy horse, they are bigger) to be. She didn't notice the glances her parents passed over the peas.

Caroline's parents sat her down on the couch in the living room. They calmly explained to her that she would not be getting a horse, and they brought out a turtle and said this would be her new pet. They asked her what she would name the turtle. Her lip quivered, and tears shot from her eyes like only a broken-hearted little girl can.

She locked herself in her room, ignoring the pleas of her parents. She stared in the mirror just crying and mumbling, "I don't want a turtle I want a horse I don't WANT a turtle I WANT a HORSE." She didn't notice the mirror start to ripple through her tears, but she saw the flash. And the half-turtle, half-horse stepped through.

By Alex Pollard
December 12, 2006 at 08:51 A.M.

This is the whale that had swallowed Pinocchio. After he had tasted the combination of wood and red overalls, he just couldn't go back to his regular diet. So every morning, at 2:45 A.M., he steps out at a random seaside village, pulls on his sweater (a hard lesson learned after getting detained for walking around naked) and goes searching for his wooden boy. And the eyes… well… just for the hell of it, I give him x-ray vision. Woohoo~

By Susan Lee | December 13, 2006 at 04:13 A.M.

Dendrobates Hypnoticus,

more commonly known as "spiked hypno-frog" (close cousin of *Futurama's* hypno-toad) is an extremely rare species found in central Australia and the only known amphibian to live in a desertic area. Amazingly, it can survive solely on moisture from its natural prey: Hymenoptera Australis, or "feathered wasp." The hunting method is one that is very rarely seen in animals, combining hypnosis and suction from its specifically adapted, triangular mouth. This particular individual is currently in captivity at Hempton Zoo in northern England and waiting for his heated enclosure to be built. The zookeepers have named him Gerald and have grown very fond of him. He has quite a personality!

By Sara Laporte | December 13, 2006 at 12:08 P.M.

Drawing:
Tuesday, 12 Dec 2006, 10:35 P.M.
Drawing posted:
Wednesday, 13 Dec 2006, 03:44 A.M.

Argus Basilicua was born of greatness. His brother helped facilitate the progress of the hybrid vehicle. His father invented the Internet. His great-aunt witnessed the signing of the No Child Left Behind Act. He was surrounded by potential. However, Argus had no drive. He had no motivation. He tried school for a number of years but was left behind in a few subjects and he never made up the credit. He tried computer programming because he wrote codes for World of Warcraft, but gave up when his Internet went down. He tried working as a gas station attendant, but hybrid cars reduced his position to twice a week.

Argus eventually found himself in his parents' basement, watching reruns of *Kate and Allie* and eating himself into a stupor. He gained around four bills and, when he could no longer get up to relieve himself, is family intervened. His mother and father pried him from his Lay-Z-Monster and forced him out.

He faltered for a few months, traveling from house to house, mooching from this friend or that, until finally, with the last of his available funds, he invested, on a whim, in 344 Design, LLC, and he was instantly rich. Stocks rose, design was back and Argus never had to worry about anything ever again.

By Brooke Nelson | December 13, 2006 at 03:18 P.M.

Well, I think I know who this monster is! He's less of an original creation; rather, he is one of many. He lives in the bowels of office supply stores (e.g., Staples, Office Max & your local store). Blogs are a food source for him, and he thrives on graduate theses, but romance novels are his favorite.

You've seen him before. He's invaded your words and mine.

His footprints, like dirty footprints in virginal snow, ruin an otherwise clean scene. Sometimes, he hides right in front of you, disguised as something so innocent as a comma,. Ah! See?! Right there he was—hiding! He's the monster of unnecessary punctuation, as well as the monster of excessive verbiage. Silently inserting himself (giggle) into writing, adding extra words, extra thoughts, muddying up writing, adding extra punctuation, making run-on sentences and extra-long lists. You can fight him with only one thing: the red-pen editing monster (who has yet to be created).

His small appendages, used to swing from line to line, adding things, eating *n*s. Rearranging the *h* & *e* in *the*. And when you thi k you catch him, he tur s i to a comma. Never to be seen. I mean, you aren't a bad writer—it's his fault! Right?

By Alex Pollard | December 14, 2006 at 08:07 A.M.

Drawing:
Tuesday, 12 Dec 2006, 10:50 P.M.
Drawing posted:
Thursday, 14 Dec 2006, 02:19 A.M.

What we have here, if I may be so bold to assume, is a prime example of a Blooper. Affectionately nicknamed in the cartooning industry for its onomatopoeia ("bloop"), it deviates erratically from the scientific name "Hairylegged Bingbangbong" (scientists everywhere were very disgruntled at the cartoonists' "childish" nickname of a very serious creature).

The Blooper is seen all too often in the cartooning field; they are sometimes found in herds gathering around the inkwell to drink, for they are in a constant state of migration. When one happens to become lost from the herd, it causes nothing but trouble for an artist should it set foot on a piece of paper. For you see, its frayed legs, resembling roots of some sort, act in the opposite manner that the roots of a plant work: Instead of taking nutrients from the environment around it, the frayed stems act as tubes for excrement. Such excrement is most unpleasant for aspiring artists, considering that with each step the Blooper takes, the liquid ink-like excrement bleeds into the paper all too easily.

By Jordan Rodrigues | December 14, 2006 at 09:54 P.M.

Little Timmy DeeDee was very rude,
always talking with a mouth full of food.
He never said thank you, you're welcome or please,
and he always kicked people's knees.

But one day, as he was walking along,
singing a little made-up song,
he saw a man in the middle of the street,
twisting about with bloody stumps for feet.

"Sir," said the man with tears in his eyes,
"A stampede of wildebeests took me by surprise,
so if you wouldn't mind helping me up from this mess,
then you shall become eternally blessed."

But Timmy just grinned and walked along,
as if nothing could ever go wrong.
But what he didn't know—that stupid little one,
was that the problems had only just begun.

For he woke up, he couldn't speak!
His beautiful lips had turned into a monstrous beak!
And to make it even worse—even though he couldn't whine,
thick black hair had grown on his spine!

And he had grown a tail like a Swiss army knife,
such a horror you've never seen in your life.
But was Timothy unhappy? Not at all!
He was so happy he could run up a wall!

Now, he thought with a gleam in his eye,
no one will dare to call me a wise guy!
They'll all be too scared to even run,
oh, this is going to be so much fun.

So nowadays, Timothy still lives,
shocks and scares are what he gives.
So remember this story, and that you see,
that is the sad fate of little Timmy DeeDee.

By Shoshana Wodinsky
December 15, 2006 at 12:01 P.M.

Drawing:
Tuesday, 12 Dec 2006, 11:05 P.M.
Drawing posted:
Friday, 15 Dec 2006, 01:52 A.M.

I am the Diamond-Sea-Cracker-Bird!
Revel in my poetry!
I am life, I am birth!
Wax me with ether so that I may
come down to earth!

(watch out for the bird, they say)

My wings are the paper, my mind the marker!

Watch out or I'll create you!
You know who you are.

(listen for the cracker, they say)

I'll crunch your numbers!
I'll eat your soul! Wax-poetic the night!

(smell the stench of the sea, they say)

Drip, drop on your head,
I'll leave my tender message.
Look up to the sky!
I am the leader, the tendon of heaven!
Connect! Connect!

(touch the diamond, they say)

I ink you to death, my red tongue
lashes your thoughts! I cut through the tape
and return what you've bought!
I am the Diamond-Sea-Cracker-Bird!
Draw me once and I become the world!!!!

By Brooke Nelson | December 15, 2006 at 06:58 P.M.

This is the Strange Error Monster of the 404ᵗʰ dimension.

It is a playful beast generally doing nothing more harmful than moving your car keys but it is still generally just a pain in the butt. It finds sustenance from stolen socks from dryers (socks must be eaten while still warm) and pens that were left in the wrong place. It lives in the colder 404th dimension and to obtain a heat source it will pop out into our dimension to steal butane lighters from people who have had a couple drinks.

The Strange Error Monster is generally regarded as a miscreant. As you can see above, it is invisible, and that makes it very hard to defend against. As with most things, we humans have to learn to live with it.

By Alex Pollard | December 16, 2006 at 08:45 A.M.

Fred Fly flew around.
Feeling flippant Fred does shout,
"Pesky human tripe!"

This was not his day.
He simply could not take it.
Fred could not feel right.

Surely understand,
Life must be hard for a fly
With an underbite.

By Sam Berkes | December 16, 2006 at 05:33 P.M.

28

Drawing:
Tuesday, 12 Dec 2006, 11:15 P.M.
Drawing posted:
Saturday, 16 Dec 2006, 03:44 A.M.

I think Da Du is probably a traveling salesman.
He sells vanilla wafers to young children so they can
turn them into liquid. The liquefied wafer goo
is then converted into energy. The energy can be used
to power villages in third world countries.
Way to go Da Du.

By Sam Berkes | December 17, 2006 at 08:31 A.M.

Drawing:
Tuesday, 12 Dec 2006, 11:30 P.M.
Drawing posted:
Sunday, 17 Dec 2006, 02:05 A.M.

Have you ever lost something dear to you?
A limb, some cheese, a trip to the zoo?
Well don't worry, it's not a lost cause,
Wiffle might have it stuffed up
within his huge schnoz.

You see, Wiffle comes from a race that's very odd,
with long stick noses and necks like a rod,
and for reasons no one can explain,
they collect more junk then a shower drain.

Inside Wiffle's nose, there's much to behold,

an old CD, some hidden gold,
a human skull, a bottle of Sprite,
a parking ticket and some kid's kite.

A bug, a fetus, lots of hairspray,
some weary traveler, old and gray,
a pair of teeth, a half-eaten pear,
my grandma and some soiled underwear.

So next time you've lost something, don't mope around,
You'll just find Wiffle dancing on the ground,
So stick your hand up there, and if you're in luck,
You'll find something in all that goopy muck.

By Shoshana Wodinsky | December 17, 2006 at 07:38 P.M.

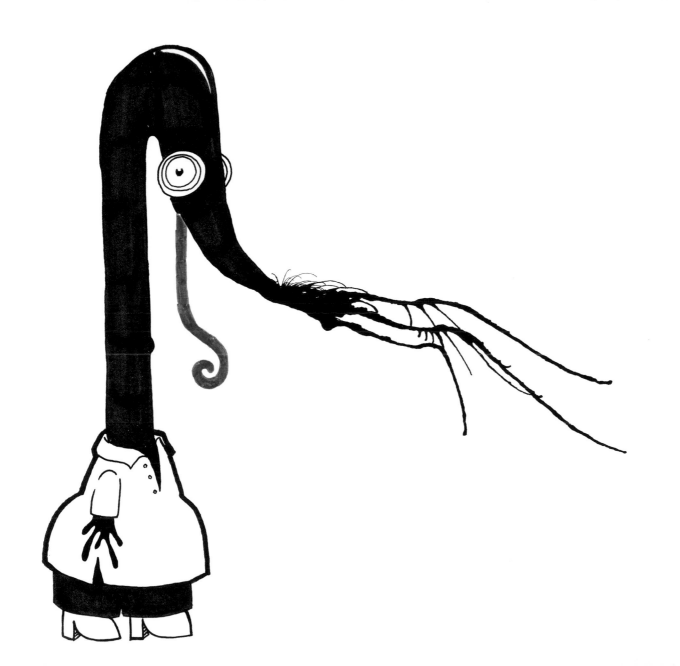

30

Drawing:
Tuesday, 12 Dec 2006, 11:45 P.M.
Drawing posted:
Monday, 18 Dec 2006, 01:43 A.M.

Today's monster has been
listening to "Placebo Headwound"
by The Flaming Lips.

By Laura Barry
December 18, 2006 at 04:12 P.M.

This is Harry Eyeball. No no, I'm not the one making the pun,

this is a forty-year-old pun, and this is where it came from.

Harry grew up in a barn in Kansas. Details are sparse on his early years, but it has been figured that he was uncomfortable at home and decided it was time to move on. Harry was walking down the highway distraught and was picked up by Stanus Alsterprix (Monster #08). Stanus understood what it meant to be an outcast, and the two drove around together in Stanus's rig for two years. They had a quiet friendship built on understanding. They both liked and hated the same things, and all in all had a good time driving together.

When they made a delivery to New York City one day Harry was smitten by the buildings and the collection of outcasts that inhabited the city. After the delivery was unloaded Harry declared, "Well, this is where I get out." "Alright. Be good little fella," Stanus replied. And that was the end of the two-year journey.

Harry, still a bit untrusting, would walk around the city and get strange stares. He saw them all. When he was particularly angry his eye would flare up (like at the end of the video).

Harry did make friends. They would sit around, have a few beers and laugh and have a good time. Harry was kind of a mean drunk and would flare up his eye whenever someone made a joke. Everyone would laugh and say, "AH! You're getting the Harry Eyeball!" This would only make Harry angrier, and make everyone laugh more, but all was forgiven by morning.

Eventually his friends started using the term in everyday speech as a term for when someone gives you a disapproving or confrontational look. It started to catch on, and since not everyone knew Harry, they thought the look was called a "Hairy Eyeball."

By Alex Pollard | December 18, 2006 at 08:14 A.M.

31

Drawing:
Monday, 18 Dec 2006, 04:45 P.M.
Drawing posted:
Tuesday, 19 Dec 2006, 03:27 A.M.

But what fish fly this way? — *Only the finest.* — Look, I know this has got to be some sort of scam, we're nearly four light years past the knorr-aPaAogl fishing zone. You really expect me to believe these aren't frozen? — *Sir, I take my work quite seriously. You can buy the fish or move on, you are holding up the line.* — Fine. Give me seven fathoms of the fl-IGGrdin naloPPnik.

Every day there was at least one like this. She wanted to put up a sign, but that would be caving to their disbelief. Nikk attracted fish. No matter where she went. It started off when she was young, she would go fishing with her father and she caught more than anyone.

Sir. We're going to have to have a word with you. — *Of course, what is it Game Warden?* — We need to see if you are using any illegal fishing equipment, it appears that you are catching quite a lot of fish, and the population is suffering as a result. — *Take a look around, but I assure you it is nothing more than my daughter's gift.* — What a beautiful eye she has. Sir, while there is no wrongdoing, we're going to have to ask you and your daughter to fish elsewhere from now on.

Nikk grew older and never really understood why she and her dad never fished anymore. She always loved fish; the ones in aquariums would always swim to her. It was kind of fun to her, she felt like the queen fish, but never really thought much of it. Then everything changed. On a vacation to jeriumTradulik she was caught in a furious lightning storm and was struck.

Doctor, will she be OK? — She will live. But from now on she will be huge, need to eat seven times a day, and now she has these funny appendages

By Alex Pollard | December 19, 2006 at 07:47 A.M.

that look like someone putting ink on paper and blowing with a cocktail straw. What are we to do? — Feed her, love her.

Nikk recovered, and so did her fish magnetism— stronger than ever. While she was still recovering at home fish started to crawl to the house. The street was littered with fish that couldn't finish the crawl, there were fish flapping on the door-step, fish slapping against the windows. People came and began to harvest the fish, but it got to a point where the trucks could not be filled up fast enough. Nikk was asked to leave for the good of the population.

So what is fresh? — *Everything.* — What is good? — *Everything.* — OK, give me that. — *Sir, you are going to have to leave.*

Nikk moved to a remote planet and settled down, her fish troubles behind her. On this planet she was regarded as one of the most beautiful women ever, just like the way she felt. She found love and settled down. But something was missing: This planet was devoid of fish. She would spend whole days thinking of fish, just wishing for one goldfish or something; she knew they missed her as much as she missed them. She wished for fish. *One day. One fish.*

It barely made the trip through space, but it made it. Nikk kept it for a few days before it died, but that one fish only made her want fish even more. And then somehow fish on other planets spontaneously mutated, were able to fly out of ponds, break orbit and fly through space toward Nikk. Only the strongest and best fish made it. So Nikk opened up a fish market.

She was happy.

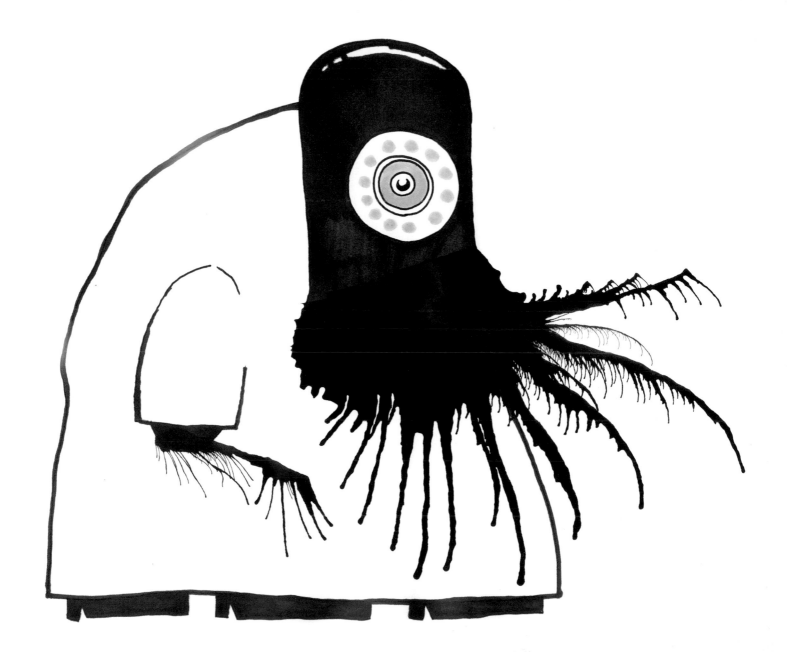

32

Unlike the Cymothoa Exigua, which removes the tongue of its host, the Lingua Sermo is not quite so bold. This individual, let's call him Parasitic Phil, acts as a tongue but never removes it. His only interaction with other species is by throwing his voice. Phil honed his skills as a ventriloquist by hiding in the mouths of the monsters he put on his shows. Although he was pretty good, he always had trouble with his m's. He idolized The Great Lester for his simplicity and wanted to be like Stroheim but never quite went crazy enough to pull it off. Eventually he settled into a routine in the mouth of a particular client, Floogle-Flip, the brother of Floogle-Flawn. Flip's mouth provided a better stage, since Flawn sported those massive choppers. Everything was going so well until Flip decided he'd had enough of Phil's freeloading ways. He chewed him up a bit to show him who was boss. Now Phil pays Flip a stipend of around 34.4 percent of his earnings. The relationship between the two has grown so well as a result.

By Sam Berkes | December 20, 2006 at 08:24 P.M.

Drawing:
Monday, 18 Dec 2006, 05:15 P.M.
Drawing posted:
Wednesday, 20 Dec 2006, 03:39 A.M.

Zzzzzzzz. Zzzzgɪɪzzzzz. Bloody 'ell, some geezas really snorin' up a storm t'night. ZZZzZzzzZkmphhhzzzz. E's going for some sorta sonic record ere, this bloke is...
It's too much! **Awright, awright. There's peoples trying to av a wee kip ere ya know. Keep it down awright guvna!?** *silence* Oh ay, maybe that was me snorin'.
I musta just fallen asleep for a wee one. *ponders* Where am I then?

I dunno, but I havtasay at least I'm all comfy like.
Least I found some posh locale to crash an all. Lookin' out for mysel an evthin.
What was I doin' befaw my nap then? *ponders* DRINKIN'!!

Shite mate, this bed is all wet. Wot av I got mysel' inna? Aw, I didn' embarass meself did ay?
Aw naw, I was drinkin' wit Georgey wanna I?
Aw naw, it's them dam fancy limoncellos gone dun me in again.
Oi, this is naught for a bed. This is some geeza's tongue I'm loungin' on!
Oh ey! I'm in Georgey's gob an all. E's been tryin' ta eat me again, the bastard.

I told im no eaten me, hundreds o' times. **I say, No eatin' me tanight Georgey, awright.**
He's as thick as two posts that Georgey. Bloody limoncellos.

But ya can't fawt the guy, really. E's got it goin' awn betta than ay. Gets the girls an' all.
Lucky bastard. I'd av it awn likesay if ay weren't unnaturally short an' all.
Diff story then I say. Unlucky draw of the straw an' all. Bloody motha nacha.

E's a good 'arted bloke, that Georgey...
if e wouldna keep tryin' ta eat a fellah, is all.

By Scott English | December 21, 2006 at 12:42 A.M.

Elroy was thrilled at the news in Monday's Page Six:
Porn-star moustaches were back, and so was co-dependency.

By Yi Shun Lai | December 21, 2006 at 08:10 A.M.

Ed was pleased with himself after watching that Jacques Cousteau video from beginning to end. There was so much information, especially about the anglerfish—did the old man say it was his cousin?—and its queer way of capturing prey. "Hey, bartender! Another round over here, please?"

By Thomas Scott | December 21, 2006 at 05:26 A.M.

Marlowe suspected that the surgery had gone horribly awry,

but he couldn't quite tell. Something was creating radio interference every time he looked at a mirror. He vaguely remembered his last words just before going under the anesthesia: "Dental implants. I want big, shiny veneers." And then, words from the doctor, who looked as if he might have consumed one too many eggnogs: "Yes. You'll look just like a reindeer, Marlowe. A big, shiny reindeer."

By Yi Shun Lai | December 21, 2006 at 05:48 P.M.

Terrance is an odd fellow. He likes Indian food. (Saag paneer is his favorite). And he has this one arm that never fully developed. The kids all called him "bug fist." It bothered him a bit, but he never let it show. When he was fourteen, his parents sent him away to military school. It was good for his self-esteem and taught him how to be tough. He volunteered for a secret military project while he was there and ended up with surveillance equipment hardwired to his brain. It never really affects him in day-to-day life, though, so he doesn't mind too much.

By Sam Berkes | December 21, 2006 at 10:01 P.M.

33

Drawing:
Wednesday, 20 Dec 2006, 10:25 P.M.
Drawing posted:
Thursday, 21 Dec 2006, 05:19 A.M.

34

We had the opportunity to sit down with Ms. Junitai Kowou on a brisk December morn. As our featured interview this month for Metro-Opulant Pediatry (MO-Ped), Ms. Kowou needs no introduction. Being a model of her talent, she literally has her foot in every door. Her talks and tours speak to the sole of the community.

JK: Something in a pump now, if you please.
[She waves the clerk to fetch the new pair while gently sipping from her coffee mug. Then she turns her attention to me to begin the interview.]

MOP: Do you remember your first pair?
JK: Without question. For the longest time, my parents wouldn't put a shoe on me. To be fair, it would have been quite expensive and we just didn't have the income. I don't fault them for that, not at all. On the contrary—my appreciation was fostered and I was immensely grateful when I got that first set. Those were the most beautiful shoes I had ever worn. Even to this day. Nothing compares. Though these pumps are looking quite the competitor.

MOP: Having not worn shoes for so long, that first pair must have been an absolute luxury. Is that what sparked your interest to become a model?
JK: Heavens no. I had no idea about such things. But I did notice that any pair I tried on seemed to be tailor made just for me. As though my feet were the mold all shoes are cast around and structured.

MOP: Clearly, you showcase them well. You won't get any argument from the writers at MO-Ped. Or our readers, for that matter. What was your most successful shoot?
JK: Oh, the spread in Posh Pheet [Spring '15 Issue]. Absolutely. Seven different shoes for that spread. It was glorious. Like I was wearing a Technicolor Dreamcoat on my feet. The photographer had this idea to show off the entire line all at once and we did it.

The world was on my feet and I was on top of the world.

By **Terry Tolleson** | December 22, 2006 at 07:37 A.M.
Read the expanded version of this story on the DVD

Emily was pleased with her new red shoes—but the wig... oh, the WIG... was enough to make any girl grin with all of her teeth.

By **Yi Shun Lai** | December 23, 2006 at 10:50 P.M.

Drawing:
Wednesday, 20 Dec 2006, 10:45 P.M.
Drawing posted:
Friday, 22 Dec 2006, 02:08 A.M.

35

His hand slapped the side of the rock face. Gripping a bulging ledge and hoisting himself up, Hankor could now see into the mouth of the enormous cave. "Perfect." This would be his new home. All Spekulars ventured out at a certain age to find their own larger caves and Hankor just found his.

Hankor pulled himself over a cropping of rock to enter the cave and surveyed his new home. It was rather moist once inside. More so than he anticipated, but a bit of a blessing. The floor had some lichen and was slippery in some spots. "Quite a wet one, I've found. Excellent!" This particular mountain zone was just on the edge of a vast desert. Having a home that was naturally cool and with some humidity in the air would provide an excellent respite for desert travelers. Upon entering the cave for shelter, they would be consumed immediately. Hankor was very pleased. "A little sprucing up here and there and it's 'Home Sweet Home'." As the giants of the land, Spekulars would either find a very large cave to lie in wait for smaller animals to venture deeper in the cave or simply appear to be their own cave.

Togdor was stirring from his slumber and blinked his eyes slowly as he awoke. After a moment, he took a look about the landscape. The desert off to the south. The rest of the mountain range behind him. "Another day," he thought to himself. He stared for several minutes, contemplating his day and then he felt it. A small padding by his lower molar. The edges of his wide-open mouth curved slightly upward with delight. Relaxing for a second, just before the entire mountain seemed to come to life. The cave entrance shook violently as Togdor closed his mouth. Hankor looked up in shock at the opening as it closed around him. "AN ANCIENT!!!! NOOOOO!!!!" Togdor grinned as he swallowed his meal while resetting his mouth. "Home Sweet Home."

By Terry Tolleson | December 23, 2006 at 08:24 A.M.
Read the expanded version of this story on the DVD

Drawing:
Wednesday, 20 Dec 2006, 10:55 P.M.
Drawing posted:
Saturday, 23 Dec 2006, 03:53 A.M.

"Alright, order please!" the announcer boomed over a slightly feedbackish microphone. "This meeting of the Twenty-eighth Chapter of the Rotten Pumpkins Prevention Society is now in session. Our first topic of discussion is this creature"—pointing to the rather large creature to his left—"who has obviously suffered from Rotten Pumpkin disease. Look at those hideously carved teeth! Now they're rotten!" The crowd oohed and aahed in amazement.

The creature, however, was in chains and handcuffs. Apparently he had been arrested off the street just to be shown at this meeting. "How dare you, fools!" he yelled. "I will eat you all up if you don't shut up at once!" The announcer seemed stunned. "Well, I mean—" "Silence! How DARE you arrest me and bring me here. You said that I was speeding!" "Well, I didn't know that—"

The creature finally lost his temper and broke out of his chains.

The audience scattered quickly as the creature made his way toward the podium where the announcer stood. The creature gave him a ponderful squint, but quickly devoured the man. "That will show him not to arrest me!" Where will this creature go next? Will he ever be forced to attend another Rotten Pumpkins Prevention Society meeting? No one will ever know!

By Ben Boatwright
December 23, 2006 at 09:41 A.M.

36

Drawing:
Friday, 22 Dec 2006, 05:30 P.M.
Drawing posted:
Sunday, 24 Dec 2006, 03:10 A.M.

I like to picture him as the Grinch that has taken some sort of strange trip to see Mt. Vesuvius. During his trip, the volcano (unbeknownst to seismologists) suddenly blew up, in a giant explosion that covered the ruins of Pompeii that had been renovated so nicely. Oops! The Grinch was caught in the middle of this eruption and so was blackened by the ash and soot that were blown out by the volcano. Why is he so happy then, you ask? Let's just say he can get a little loony in that straightjacket (that is what he's wearing, isn't it?).

By Ben Boatwright | December 24, 2006 at 10:04 A.M.

Bizzaro Santa.
Surreal in his red hat.
He scares me sometimes.

By Sam Berkes | December 24, 2006 at 09:24 P.M.

Whoa! Santa looks rough after those all-night benders!

By Terry Tolleson | December 24, 2006 at 11:01 P.M.

I gots four eyes that burn. They burn like fire. They could really be laser beams, but I don't like to talk about that, because someone might steal 'em and then my eyes would nots be in my head anymore. I gots this hat with fluff on it. It's like cotton, but different. It helps me to keep my balance when I drinks too much bourbon. I gots these stringy things for teeth. I like 'em. Sometimes they gets tangled and I gots to use conditioner on 'em so that I can comb 'em out. Everybody's always making fun of me abouts my teeth, but I just says I like 'em and I don't wants to be hearing all that mess. They better watch whats they says to me, I might just gets angry and use my laser beam eyes. That'd show 'em.

By **Stephanie Knauss** | December 25, 2006 at 12:35 P.M.

After his run-in with Mt. Vesuvius, the radioactive particles thrown far into the atmosphere caused the Grinch to grow two additional eyes, which now have superlaser capabilities! That even rivals the great Zeus on Vesu— oh wait, that's Olympus. Never mind then.

On a side note, I received a "Daily Monster Kit" for Christmas that had been constructed by Mom—a bottle of black ink, straws, and two Sharpies. Thanks for the inspiration!

By **Ben Boatwright** | December 25, 2006 at 05:35 P.M.

The tar-bearded Santa had a rough night delivering all the presents around the world. When he finally got home he had gone so nuts from all of that craziness he miraculously grew two extra eyes! And then started bleeding from them... more on that later.

By **Azalea Mayes** | December 26, 2006 at 12:05 A.M.

They called me "four eyes" in high school.
That was before I ate them.
See that stuff between my teeth?
That's them.

By **Yi Shun Lai** | December 26, 2006 at 07:32 A.M.

Drawing:
Friday, 22 Dec 2006, 05:50 P.M.
Drawing posted:
Monday, 25 Dec 2006, 02:16 A.M.

You need to see my qualifications? I'll tell you: I'm a showgirl by trade, an entertainer at heart. I've got my own costume and everything, but you'll need to build me a pool to perform in. What? No, I wouldn't rather go see if those freaks over at Cirque du Soleil have an opening, thank you very much! Yes, yes, I know everything in that show "O" is done in water— but I don't speak no freakin' Canadian. What? Oh, thank you. You know, if you hadn't given me the job just now I'd have had to beat you severely about the groin with my wading appendages.

By Yi Shun Lai | December 26, 2006 at 07:49 A.M.

It was a cool autumn afternoon at the Gatekeeper pond. Franklin enjoyed his after-lunch swim this day, like he did every day. The wind was mild and the water was just perfect. He smiled to himself as he paddled around, admiring all the changing leaves, basking in the sunlight.

BEEP! BEEP! BEEP!

Suddenly the warning beeps from his battery pack went off. Realizing that he only had sixteen seconds until his Auto Legs lost power, he began to panic. I will be stuck in the middle of the pond forever!! he silently screamed in his head. What will I do then!?

Out of the corner of his eye he spotted a shiny cylindrical object in the grasses on the shore. A battery!! Go Auto Legs! Go, go, go! he demanded of his mechanical legs. With only seconds to go before he lost the use of his legs, he got to the shore and swallowed the battery. Oh, if only Franklin could read.

Franklin now sits, dead in the water, unable to swim or paddle. He tells stories to passersby; tales of Auto Legs and afternoon swims. He reminds himself of the good old days when he could move about freely. Poor Franklin, unable to move, for what he thought was a battery was a can of Bud Light. And now, he sits in the middle of Gatekeeper pond with that can lodged in his throat and no power to move his Auto Legs. Poor, poor Franklin.

By Stephanie Knauss | December 26, 2006 at 05:03 P.M.

Drawing:
Friday, 22 Dec 2006, 06:13 P.M.
Drawing posted:
Tuesday, 26 Dec 2006, 01:04 A.M.

39

Drawing:
Friday, 22 Dec 2006, 06:25 P.M.
Drawing posted:
Wednesday, 27 Jan 2007, 12:59 A.M.

Johanssen peered out with a nervous eye. It was still there. Floating across the lawn. Thousands of years and natural selection had made the hideous tormentor more treacherous. Stronger. Quicker. Faster. Airborne. Before, moving homes high up into the trees was a surefire method of survival from the beast. Now, it was only a matter of time before one would find colonies and devour entire families. Nary a survivor. "We're stuck. There's no way out and it'll find the colony soon, for sure," uttered Johanssen to the other workers. A strapping young worker responded, "What of the soldiers? Can't they help?" "Are you serious, Henrickson?! Look at the size of that thing. Our soldiers' attacks would be but a pin prick to that monstrosity," replied another.

Johanssen had to think of a plan. Most of the workers looked to him for guidance. He gave a shallow breath and faced everyone. "OK… there is an outside chance it won't realize we're here. Maybe it won't notice the colony and will move on. There is a nice watering hole down there and it may just be taking a moment to refresh itself." "You just said it would find us for sure!" retorted a panicked worker. "Hey! Ya! WE'RE DOOMED!!!" shrieked another. Johanssen needed a plan, now more than ever. They couldn't outrun it. There was no way to divert its attention. The nearest colony was quite a long way off, so help from them would be out of the question.

AAAAAAAAAAAAHHHHHHHHHH! IT'S SEEN US!!!!

came the screams of the workers. They scattered in confused patterns with many just heading outside, without concern of the consequences. The animal hurled itself up the tree, slamming into the colony walls. Ripping them open. Huge chunks of debris with workers and soldiers hurtling toward the ground. Then its tongue shot out of its long snout—lashing at the ants for a hearty meal, lapping them up, hundreds at a time. Johanssen was about to turn a corner when the sticky, wet tentacle smacked his back. He screamed in terror as he was ripped from his home. He spied Henrickson gazing, in horror, back at him from below. His last vision being that of his friend being crushed under the spindly appendage that destroyed the colony to feast on its helpless inhabitants.

By Terry Tolleson | December 27, 2006 at 09:10 A.M.
Read the expanded version of this story on the DVD

"It's off to the races yet again today, folks! Yes, the odds are 5-2 on this one, it looks like a real racer. That extendable snout always seems to get him the win out here at the Monstucky Derby. And they're off! Down the front stretch, it looks like—oh my! The three-legged snoutster has tripped over himself and fallen straight into the dirt! Ouch! But what's this!? He's stuck out his extendable snout and tripped every other one of the monster racers! What an upset, ladies and gentlemen! Here he goes, running around the track. Here he comes to the finish line… and #39 wins it again, by a huge margin!" The Monstucky Derby—my favorite in the Triple Crown series.

By Ben Boatwright | December 27, 2006 at 12:14 P.M.

Shirley Temple
Are you an octopus on skis?
Aspen called
Daddy Warbucks made you boots
Are you happy?

By Alex Pollard | December 28, 2006 at 07:18 A.M.

It's a little-known fact that 40 is actually from Morgedal, Norway... the city in which ski jumping originated. Unable to compete in the first competition in 1862, he's been practicing for more than a century and will soon compete in the Ski-flying hill competition (the most extreme version of all ski jumping) at Holycowurcrazy Hill, in mid-February of 2007.

Due to amazing agility, his wire-thin frame and nearly weightless head (hey you don't need brains to fly over two hundred meters into the air), he's successfully mastered this sport and is sure to win the grand prize... nothing less than to be awarded with free Wheaties for life will do for this soon-to-be-famous champion.

By Amy Fedele | December 28, 2006 at 10:32 A.M.

Indeed, this is no skiing event, but the newest revolution in aircraft technology. This fine alien is modeling our newest concoction:

THE 140-SX SKILINER.™

Anyone can get on the skis and take off into the air for a great time! Fly as high and fast as you want—you can even fly around all day.

DISCLAIMER: Maximum altitude of one hundred meters. Do not attempt while eating, drinking, smoking or consuming alcohol. Never operate machinery, including the 140-SX Skiliner™, while drinking any alcoholic beverages. Do not exceed speeds of over 50 km/h. If maximum speed is exceeded, the one-year limited warranty becomes null and void. Skiliner™ may experience sudden shifts in direction and speed, which could lead to serious injury or death. Maximum battery life of fifteen minutes. Battery failure may cause crashing of the vehicle, which could also result in serious injury or death. People or aliens with heart, neck or back problems should not attempt to ride the 140-SX Skiliner™. Also, people under the age of fourteen should not ride the Skiliner™. The Skiliner Corporation does not assume any liability for losses or damages incurred while using this product.

By Ben Boatwright | December 28, 2006 at 10:50 A.M.

Drawing:
Friday, 22 Dec 2006, 06:50 P.M.
Drawing posted:
Thursday, 28 Jan 2007, 01:01 A.M.

Well, she is a dancer, from the Folies-Bergère, in the days
of the Belle Époque. She is so happy you revived her.
Since she has just been woken up, her hair is a little disheveled.
But wait until she starts dancing! With four legs that definitely
can be lengthened up, the spectacle will be magnificent!

By Selma Tischler | December 29, 2006 at 09:32 A.M.

This is the revered inspector #41.

His nametag graces the likes of leather gloves, socks and sometimes shoes.
Starting as inspector 344, he has worked his way up the corporate ladder.
Soon, he will be #1, and things will really start happening for him.

By Sam Berkes | December 29, 2006 at 11:27 P.M.

"Oh no, that's a common misconception"…"Yes, you see, you are mistaken.
Filled with propaganda about the number 42 being the meaning of Life,
the Universe and Everything. And I'll have you know that rat-bastard #42
has been none too quick about clearing up the confusion either"…
grumbles incomprehensibly…"Why, I should whap him upside the head
I should!" *nods* "Get some sense into that miscreant.

It should be ME, #41, in the limelight! Me, the evolution of pure DNA,
the epitome of the biological struggle. Carbon perfection incarnate.
Look, I can even do this neat little jig!"

By Scott English | December 29, 2006 at 11:41 P.M.

Drawing:
Friday, 22 Dec 2006, 07:10 P.M.
Drawing posted:
Friday, 29 Dec 2007, 12:01 A.M.

"Thank Brach for Brach!" They say on the small planet of Mervis.
It is the great Brach from whom all life flows.

The world of Mervis is an odd one, spinning for a Mervian year in a counterclockwise motion,
then for a Mervian year in a clockwise motion and so repeating for all eternity,
or until the great Brach tires of their world.

The planet's surface, of a red pigment, is made of concentric valleys and mountains circling
to the capital city of Entil. The people of Entil's sole purpose is to continue the spinning
of the planet so that Brach will not be displeased and tire quickly of the planet. These dedicated
souls work round-the-clock to ensure the planet's consistent spin in the current direction.
Their most important job falls on The Day of Change, the Mervian New Year, when all citizens
of the city must use a personal bicycle pedal-like instrument to aid in the reversal
of the planet's spin.

Unfortunately for the Mervians Brach tires quickly and about every twenty to fifty Mervian
years Brach throws the planet haphazardly across the universe. Few survive the impact
and those who do fall into a deep slumber until Brach chooses to revitalize the planet
and the cycle begins again.

The Mervians, the worshippers of Brach, would be glad to know that despite Brach's
disaffection with the unceasing continuation of life on Mervis, it remains his choice planet
and he will always return, bringing forth the Day of Glory. A day spent entirely
in worship of the all-seeing eye.

By Kyle J. Britt | December 30, 2006 at 12:26 A.M.

Drawing:
Friday, 22 Dec 2006, 07:30 P.M.
Drawing posted:
Saturday, 30 Dec 2006, 12:02 A.M.

Before anyone discovered the scientific method for or suffered the repercussions
of busting open atoms, Sigmund Koppel, aka The Supplanter, won the local
yo-yo competition in the "Split the Atom" category. In fact, his great-great-great
times fifty-two grandfather invented the trick. The Koppels are of an incredibly
old and venerated monster lineage, older even than the oldest testament written.
They live secretly among us; are very shy, peaceable and fond of numerology;
adore latkes with chopped liver; and speak mostly in tandem palindromes.
A typical Koppel greeting one to another:

They are true mensches, all, and yo-yos are their favorite tchotchkes.

By Victoria Koldewyn | December 30, 2006 at 06:02 P.M.

Monster 43 should be afraid of Monster 44, who is hiding this ominous little box somewhere in his tummy! What is in there? Explosives? Nah! Poison? Maybe! A little radioactive substance? Ah, yeah… more probable!

By Selma Tischler | December 31, 2006 at 07:05 A.M.

Drawing:
Friday, 22 Dec 2006, 08:10 P.M.
Drawing posted:
Sunday, 31 Dec 2006, 12:01 A.M.

Dear Mr. Johnson,

Due to the nature of your management style, unfavorable office lighting, lack of a snack bar and overall unsatisfactory working conditions, I am leaving my position as Roving Office Monkey. I have enjoyed the job for these six years, but, as much as I enjoyed the position, I cannot tolerate the environment any longer.

As pointed out by myself in our company meeting on Monday, there is a serious need for snacks in this company. I have yet to understand how you think we can work all day, to our fullest abilities, without proper snacks. It is unfair and downright silly to think we can accomplish all of our daily tasks without snacks.

Also, the eyestrain caused by the poor lighting is enough to send one to bed for a week. Some days I thought my eyes would begin to bleed. They didn't, mind you, but they could have.

I know it is the end of the year, and this will probably come as a shock, my leaving. But it has to be done, for my sanity and for the sake of my need for snacks.

My desk is cleared out and you will not see me in this office again. I wish you all the best, Mr. Johnson, in the upcoming year.

Sincerely,

Ronald P. Forty, III

Later that day, in Mr. Johnson's office:

"SNACKS!" bellowed Mr. Johnson. "That silly little monster is leaving because of SNACKS?" Mr. Johnson ran his hand over his ridiculously large face, being careful to not get his fingers caught in his tentacle-like bottom teeth. It had been a rough day. This end-of-the-year crap was really starting to get to him. The Boss Boss was breathing down his neck about the low numbers, his wife was threatening to leave him if he missed another New Year's toast and now he had lost his Office Monkey because of dim lights and no snacks! Could it be any worse??

Sighing to himself, he got up from his desk and headed for the door. There was nothing he could do tonight other than drink some champagne and eat finger food. It would all have to wait until next year. THE END!

By Stephanie Knauss | December 31, 2006 at 02:10 P.M.

Some people say that change is good.
They don't know what it's like, to have it be out of your control.

I had these lovely gamine legs, you see, the sort of things a Rockette might envy.
And they were taken away, and instead I have this bizarre pear-shaped body, now.
And then there was this briefcase. A nice vachetta-type one, with a sturdy handle,
that I carried all of my manuscripts in, but that, too, was taken away.

I'm only smiling because he gave me a tail. It was long, at first, and I liked that,
but then he added extra fronds, and I think I like that better. It's like when
people at the hairdresser ask for layers? You know, more body? Yeah, like that.

Maybe they're right. Maybe change is for the better.

By Yi Shun Lai | January 02, 2007 at 12:46 P.M.

Drawing:
Friday, 22 Dec 2006, 08:30 P.M.
Drawing posted:
Sunday, 31 Dec 2006, 12:01 A.M.

Bernie and Erica loved each other so,
But they would never stop fighting, to and fro.
You see, Erica was a gal that liked fun,
But her husband Bernie was always on the run.

"Sweetie," whined Erica in her annoying tone,
"You're always in a meeting or on the phone!
Can't you just take a break from being so businessey,
And come out to go roller skating with me?"

Well, Bernie devised the best plan he could.
To get rid of that annoying girl for good.
So he put glue in her skates, encasing her toes,
How she'll get out of that, nobody knows.

But Bernie didn't care, he just laughed!
He didn't even notice the sudden updraft,
That sent his wife into a downhill spin,
In which she landed right on top of him.

So she crushed him beneath her weight,
Now that's what I call a gruesome fate.
But he still has that face of glee,
Planted on for all to see.

By Shoshana Wodinsky | December 31, 2006 at 09:22 P.M.

Drawing:
Friday, 22 Dec 2006, 09:05 P.M.
Drawing posted:
Monday, 01 Jan 2007, 12:01 P.M.

J. Peter Malton was retiring today. This was the last run. Nothing crazy. Narton Valley's best product. Pride of the system. He wasn't kidding himself, however; it wasn't one of his normal high-profile deals. Which was good, no one would really concern themselves with a haul of this nature. This shipment would be a breeze—just what a retiring guy wanted. He'd done enough of these kinds of hauls to know what to do. The freighter sliced through the Orfeáte Nebula, coasting on the low grid, when the proximity alarm blared.

Malton shot up in the chair and switched over to manual. "Last day…" he sighed. It shot out of a thick patch of dust and particles. A small, nondescript cruiser. "Well, well. Come to play, have ya?" He rolled the freighter hard to the right. Three times the size of the cruiser, it could take the hit. "I know what you are and you ain't alone, you sonofa…" The cruiser pulled up sharply, skimming the top of the freighter. It twisted around and then dove sharp into another cloudy patch. "Tricky, tricky. They've found me for sure. Question is, how to get out? Two holds… now wouldn't that be some good irony…" Malton grinned and thumbed a switch.

"I have you now! All units—flight path coordinates are being transmitted. Converge on my mark."

The captain of the interceptor slapped a hand on the ensign's shoulder. "Been after this bastard for years. Finally caught up with him. Open a channel, ensign!" A short pause. "Jacob Peter Malton, aka Malt 40, this is Inspector Davidson. No need for the formalities: The nebula is quite surrounded.

Your stolen freighter has nowhere to go. It's over."

"I'll hand it to ya for trackin' me, Inspector. But ain't no way I'm done here. Not by you." Even with the interference Davidson could still hear the smile across Malt's face. "Sir! I got bogeys all over the comm. Must be around two hundred of them, easy, swarming all over the place!" the ensign shouted. The detective's eyes got wide. "Get in there! I want him now!" All the ships burst through the nebula. "Main screen!" Davidson's spirits dropped as the space before his ship came into view. They couldn't track him. Too much interference. Too much "debris."

"You clever son of a bitch," was Davidson's response as he stared at hundreds of Narton Valley's best floating in front of him. "Goddamn pigs. He stole a freighter full of pigs." Malton's voice cracked over the frequency one last time, "It's my last day. Breakfast's on me. I smell bacon."

By Terry Tolleson | January 01, 2007 at 10:16 P.M.
Read the expanded version of this story on the DVD

Things went haywire one evening on the set of *Space Truckers* when one of the gaffers decided to have some fun. He thought it would be amusing to feed one of the square pigs an antigravity beer to see what would happen. He had no idea it would cause so much damage to the orthogonal swine. It inflated outward like a blowfish, with its razorback coat soaring toward the ceiling. The guilty gaffer was looking at six to eight for animal cruelty, but everything was golden when it was found the pig reformed after the suds passed through its system. Let this be a lesson to you: Never fuel foursquare feral pork full of floatable ale. Nothing good can come of it.

By Sam Berkes | January 01, 2007 at 10:45 P.M.

Looks like a horsequito!

By Capt. Robert Emmet Coogan, USMC | January 02, 2007 at 08:11 A.M.

46

Drawing:
Friday, 22 Dec 2006, 08:45 P.M.
Drawing posted:
Tuesday, 02 Jan 2007, 01:08 A.M.

Look, up in the sky—it's National Velvet, it's Seabiscuit—no, it's the Flying Donkman! Flying over the city, seeking out crime wherever it may be!

By Ben Boatwright
January 02, 2007 at 12:01 P.M.
Read the expanded version of this story on the DVD

JOHN STOCKTON: We're back and we'll check with Chet Peterson in a moment for the weather, but now...I'm being told it will be over to Bob first... it's the Day After New Year's Day Parade here in lovely Weippe, Idaho—the Marty's Hardware and Pizzeria's Parade. As with every year, free cases of ten-penny nails and all-you-can-eat calzones. We're going to Bob, who's joining us now from somewhere in the middle of that parade. Hey, Bob, things are shaping up rather nicely.

BOB HEFTER: You know what? Actually, I can talk about the weather, because as you know, John, I've been doing this for several years now. It never changes. It's cold. Really cold. Why is it so damn cold, you ask? Because we live in Idaho. And it's January. Look! Snow! Who didn't see that coming?

SELMA RODRIGUEZ, parade goer: Absolutely. Get us up every day after New Year's Day morning and we had to sit there in front of the television and watch the parade. He wanted our family to know what it was like in the old country. You see, balloon #46...

BOB: Howdy Horsey?

SELMA: Yeah. That one. My father's father was mauled by a wild herd of those things and he wanted all of us to know the dangers of giant balloons.

BOB: Wait, you mean mauled by wild horses, right? That's truly... weird.

SELMA: No—mauled by a wild pack of those giant balloon animals you guys are escorting down the streets. *[Camera cut to Bob, whose mouth is wide open as he stands in complete confusion.]*

SELMA: True story. *[Awkward silence.]*

BOB: John... back to you. Forever. Happy New Year, ya freaks.

By Terry Tolleson | January 02, 2007 at 11:31 A.M.
Read the expanded version of this story on the DVD

47

Das says I oughtn't smile like I do. He says a good monster doesn't ever, ever smile. But if I didn't smile, no one would ever see what's caught between my teeth, and then how would they know what I've eaten? Das always think that good monsters shouldn't have any fun, don't you think? Today's repast was a wee bairn of a giant. Bone-crunching-liscious it was, and don't you think a monster ought to smile at such a meal?

By Yi Shun Lai | January 03, 2007 at 10:24 A.M.

Drawing:
Friday, 22 Dec 2006, 09:15 P.M.
Drawing posted:
Wednesday, 03 Jan 2007, 04:00 A.M.

Rare, tranquil and quite ferocious, the flying hammerhead squirrel has been pushed to the brink of extinction. People hunted the poor creatures for their delicate tail plumage, as well as their uniquely shaped skulls. The only known species of flying hammerhead squirrel is thought to be surviving in northern Idaho near Lake Pend Oreille.

For as little as ninety-four cents a day, you can help these struggling creatures. Just send your pledge check of 344 dollars to:

The Endangered Hammerhead Squirrel Prevention Center
2345 Box Spring Road
Sandpoint, ID 83809

Thanks in advance for your kindness.

P.S.: Although the flying hammerhead squirrel may look kind and gentle (they do smile an awful lot), they are vicious creatures that will rip your eyes out if given the chance. Please take cover if you see one flying toward your head. And again, thanks for your kindness.

By Sam Berkes | January 03, 2007 at 09:42 P.M.

Today, Monster 48 seems to be standing on his tiptoes. Ah yes, the old tiptoe tap dance. It used to be rather popular back in the 4500s, but now since it's year 4617 for old Monster 48, he seems a bit... out of style, I'm afraid. Those pinstripe pants are still stylin'! Nevertheless, the ISP (In-Style Police) may be after him pretty soon if he keeps up his act. He still seems to be making a good amount of money off of it—thirty-four π per show.

By Ben Boatwright | January 04, 2007 at 05:55 A.M.

I knew it: My dad's eyebrow has finally walked off on its own. (No, seriously.)

By Yi Shun Lai | January 04, 2007 at 08:28 A.M.

Drawing:
Friday, 22 Dec 2006, 09:30 P.M.
Drawing posted:
Thursday, 04 Jan 2007, 01:47 A.M.

Though the monsters of this species (*Beastie shape-shifterum*) are recognizable by virtually anyone born on this continent—and why wouldn't they be?—they are the most skilled and socially celebrated accountants. What is not commonly known is that their "outfits" are really the natural markings and contours of their fascinating physiognomy.

As this species slowly began to mesh their culture with that of the humans, they adapted their bodies in order to protect themselves while developing a mutually beneficial relationship with the human culture. This amphibious Beastie species, while unable to shape-shift in the "magical" manner, are able to use water to completely change how they look. Their bristling "fur" (really a dense carpet of hair and fleshy polyps) flattens under the weight of water, rather like a cat's might, with the added biologic bonus of changing color. So a hunted Beastie shapeshifterum (a tasty snack for birds of prey, city rodents and a rare species of giant spider) need only make it

to a water source to change from a black fluffy-haired creature to a skinny long-haired purple one. They started to turn their bristling coats inwards proportionally with their acceptance into human society, so that now they look like they are wearing fur-lined coats. They cannot turn their hides completely inside out—they must have at least 25 percent of their natural coat exposed to air and light—so they desperately hope fur does not go out of fashion and naturally are one of the top lobbying groups for the fur industry. The "pinstripe pants" are gills that allow them to breathe underwater and the "shoes" are really their heads, each "eyelet" an eye, the "laces" exocortical neurons and the "heels" a set of cerebellums. What most people take for their eyes is a simple matter of that most basic of natural survival tricks—mimicry. These "eyes" are their hearing and olfactory organs.

The ethics of a species having to physically adapt so dramatically in order to fit in with another species' culture is a current hot topic of debate.

By Adriane Bovone | January 04, 2007 at 11:53 A.M.

After the upset victory over the Mortuary State Cadavers the students of Crematorium Tech rushed the field. In the celebratory hysteria that followed two players were injured, four cheerleaders went missing and both goalposts were torn down and dismantled. (Weeks later the goalposts would be found for bid on eBay, along with one of the cheerleaders.)
With the championship game in two weeks…

Coach Growler knew he had a big problem.

His solutions were limited. In an act of desperation he offered full scholarships to the Einstein twins. Surprised, they immediately accepted, as they felt honored to be part of such a proud tradition.

Their excitement was to be short-lived as they stepped onto the football field and Coach positioned them ten yards deep in the end zone. "The goalposts won't be fixed for a month. Now stand there and don't move. And try not to get hurt. Go Flamers!"

By Bill Bibo Jr. | January 05, 2007 at 07:40 A.M.

Drawing:
Friday, 22 Dec 2006, 10:10 P.M.
Drawing posted:
Friday, 05 Jan 2007, 02:38 A.M.

Life as a thistle is loads of fun, sure—IF YOU'RE NOT SHARING A STALK WITH SOMEONE. Look, it's not even that we have two heads. We're two completely different PLANTS. We know, we know, it's weird. But we think differently, we talk differently, we even accessorize differently. This stupid sweatshirt? So not my idea. Shut up, Frank. Wipe that silly grin off your face. Stop tickling us. I mean it. STOP IT STOP IT STOP IT STOP—

By Yi Shun Lai | January 05, 2007 at 12:25 P.M.

The seventies brought forth many great triumphs: The Ford Pinto was first introduced, Mozambique gained independence from Portugal and a small but monumental film from director Lee Frost was unleashed upon us. Satchel was all set to play a major part in Frost's masterpiece, *The Thing With Two Heads,* but got blacklisted at the last minute. Turns out he didn't quite mesh with the other actors, what with his poor dental hygiene and the fact that he was a Twins fan.

Now he spends his time selling toasted almonds on street corners and looking for extra work where he can. He shares a studio apartment with six other out-of-work actors in south Hollywood. Life is pretty good, though, for a guy with two heads.

By Sam Berkes | January 05, 2007 at 10:34 P.M.

Monster #50, Darshan Featherbottom, is the kind of fellow who enjoys a party. But flashing lights and disco ball reflections really irritate his beak-eyes. Fortunately, millions of years of evolution have been kind to Darshan. Whenever he feels the need to sheath his peepers all he has to do is blink and a thin fibrous membrane, not unlike human fingernails, covers them up so no light can shine through. Now if he could only do something about his excessive down plumage, he'd be set.

By **Sam Berkes** | January 2006, 2007 at 03:00 P.M.

Drawing:
Friday, 22 Dec 2006, 10:35 P.M.
Drawing posted:
Saturday, 06 Jan 2007, 02:36 A.M.

Name: .... Farsighted Forsythe
Special Talent: .... precognition
Age: .... half an Earth century
Favorite Song: .... "Yellow Submarine"
Vision: 20-20-20-20-20-20
Preferred Mode of Transportation: .... by camelback (oddly enough)

By **Victoria Koldewyn** | January 2006, 2007 at 09:08 P.M.

Oh yeah. I been training these li'l fellers for about... going on ten years now. Yup. These things really are a special breed. Differen 'en most other of them thangs you can get down in Port Scanton. Most folks'll tell ya that it's cuz of that set of power lines over yonder that gives 'em the extra eyes. I thinks it's advanced. Y'know— what's tha' word... revolved? I dunno. I'll say it's a bit creepy when they blink though. It makes an awful, sticky sound cuz them lids'll close all at once. Gives me the crawlies. But I deal with it, traveling from town to town with this here circus.

We travel and put on shows. Yup. People come watch them and they watch the people. They always watching. Watching and not makin' a peep. Just watchin.' With all them eyes. Lookin' at the people as they walk by. They loves kids. Always hop up and down the perches when them come up to take a peep. Guess they loves the attention. What's tha'? No, I don't know anything 'tal 'bout all them missing kid stories tha' been goin' round.

By **Terry Tolleson** | January 2006, 2007 at 10:57 P.M.
Read the expanded version of this story on the DVD

51

So on Monday morning, I opened the clinic, like I always do. I had no sooner grabbed my coffee **when this guy comes in and starts gasping something about a zucchini.** And I thought, "Oh sure, and me without the squash extractor even set up yet."

By **Annie Nordmark** | January 07, 2007 at 08:45 A.M.

Drawing:
Sunday, 07 Jan 2007, 12:52 A.M.
Drawing posted:
Sunday, 07 Jan 2007, 04:00 A.M.

Meet Dominick. He's the world's smallest watchmaker.
Most people think he's Swiss, but I know the real truth.
He grew up in South Chicago, took a few classes on watch making, and just went with it. He's only about a foot tall, so his wee little hands can get into some small places.
His metal of choice used to be copper until a fateful smelting accident that left his tongue horribly disfigured.
Its solid copper now, and colored green as a result.
Poor Dominick. Luckily, he's a great craftsman.

By **Sam D. Berkes** | January 07, 2007 at 08:15 P.M.

Most of the gumshoes at Tattletale PI prefer grape popsicles. But Florentine here prefers lime-wasabi. Flo is suffering from brain freeze sinus 'splosion, having just gobbled a six-pack. (Suffering is actually a misrepresentation... Flo derives great gustatory pleasure from these made-to-order confections.)

By **Victoria Koldewyn** | January 07, 2007 at 10:35 P.M.

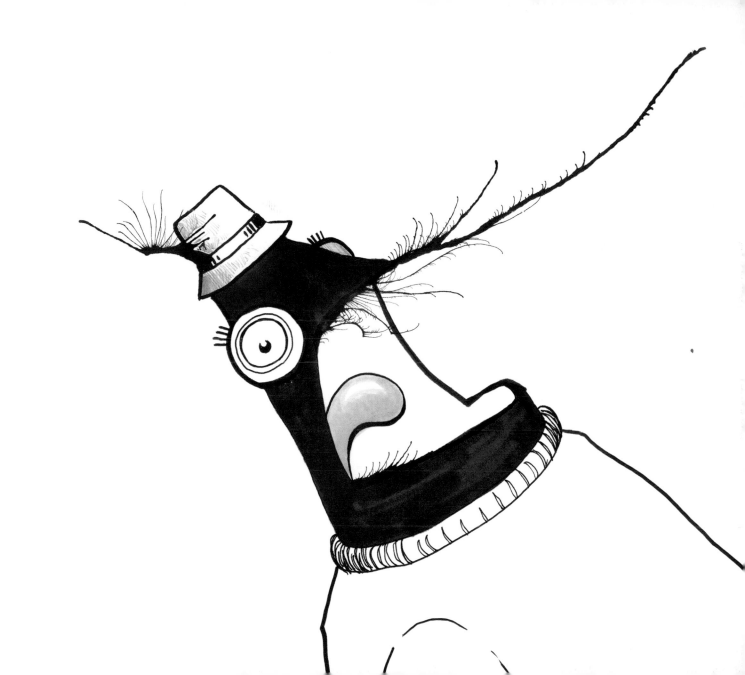

They call him Waylon, Waylon the Smiling Executioner. It's not that he was particularly happy about executing people... not that he wasn't, it's just that as a child his face got stuck in an awkward—well, awkwardly happy countenance, sadly dashing any hopes he had for a career in broadcasting. So, he trained in the one vocation he thought he might enjoy that would allow him to hide behind a mask—Disney, of course, never sent recruiters to his school.

He went to the DeFry School of Executioning, majoring in the hanging arts.

After years of tying knots and tossing rope, today was his day to shine. "Don't blow it, Waylon," he thought. And as he stood there, warming up the crowd with a few of his best ice-breaking jokes, he knew he had them in the palm of his hand, and this was what he was born to do.

By Pimpom Tomlinson | January 08, 2007 at 09:28 A.M.

Drawing:
Sunday, 07 Jan 2007, 01:05 A.M.
Drawing posted:
Monday, 08 Jan 2007, 02:42 A.M.

When someone comes up to you, brandishing a weapon and telling you to order another round—for your health—you do it. "Awfully risky showing your face here, dontcha think, kid?" came the drink requisitioner's rough statement. "Not exactly hard to pick you out of a crowd these days. You know how much is on your head? What do you think your chances are of getting out of this joint alive?" He patted his right side as he asked the latter.

"I don't care. I got other, more pressing issues to deal with." Arthur kept staring straight at the shelves of booze lining the back wall. He placed a hand to the back of his head and pulled along his shaggy ponytail. Turning to face the gun-toting individual, Arthur looked to make a slight jerking motion, which happened in a blink of an eye. He raised his hand to examine the item it now held. "And, old man, I'd say my chances are better than average." The old man gave a wry smile and started to chuckle under his breath as he felt to ensure his gun was, in fact, no longer in his possession. "Always with the bravado, boy. Just remember, that gun has a tricky guidance system. Better know what you're doing or the damn ammo will blow only three feet from you." He placed a hand on Arthur's shoulder and stood up. Arthur tucked the pistol under his sweater, and signalled for another drink. "Thanks, Dad. Here's to you giving me more advice in the future."

By Terry Tolleson | January 08, 2007 at 12:25 P.M.
Read the expanded version of this story on the DVD

This is Cheech and Chong's cousin Chin, from Downundah. Now Earth monsters' chins in the northern hemisphere, they protrude in a downward fashion. Monsters from Downundah, their chins jut upward. See everything is backwards and opposite. Chin, like his cousins, enjoys the finer things in life. A good cigar, say. Maybe that's why he's looking so punchy pleased. And why everything's so upsidey downsey.

By Victoria Koldewyn | January 08, 2007 at 04:00 P.M.

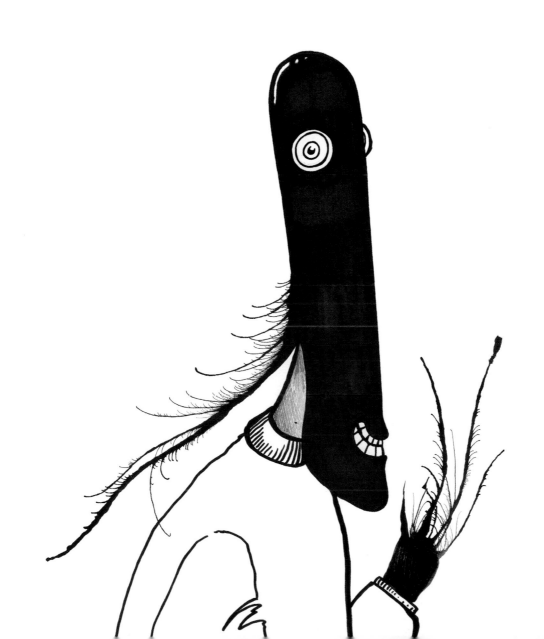

Just think, with an eye like that, you could perform your own esophagogastroduodenoscopy!

By Thaddeus Quintin | January 09, 2007 at 07:20 A.M.

He's the grilled cheese monster. This is how I know:

1. He walks around with his mouth open.
2. He's scary looking so people feed him.
3. What is more yummy than grilled cheese?
4. He has an eye coming from his stomach.
   What would the eye be looking for? Yummy things! *(See #3)*

By Alex Pollard | January 09, 2007 at 09:06 A.M.

Cleveland loved it when Archie rode his motorcycle with his mouth open. He could feel the wind whipping through his hair—the freedom he felt. For just those few moments it was as if he wasn't tethered to the tonsils.

When he'd applied to sidekick school, he had a more conventional career in mind. He was prepared to wear tights, answer phones or ride shotgun, but live in someone's mouth? That wasn't in the brochure.

By Pimpom Tomlinson | January 09, 2007 at 03:55 P.M.

Meet Guy Snockerly, host of the wildly popular game show *Win Monster Money*, and his faithful sidekick Ebberts. Monster fans love *Win Monster Money*, which requires its contestants first to answer tricky riddles posed by sidekick Ebberts. For every right answer, a monster contestant chooses one hapless groundling out of a nearby pit to be spun on the Wheel of Fun. The monster whose groundling lasts the longest wins the big prize, $200,000 and a lifetime supply of Monster Floss, personally recommended by Guy Snockerly himself.

By Juliet Williams | January 09, 2007 at 09:35 P.M.

Drawing:
Sunday, 07 Jan 2007, 01:30 A.M.
Drawing posted:
Tuesday, 09 Jan 2007, 03:18 A.M.

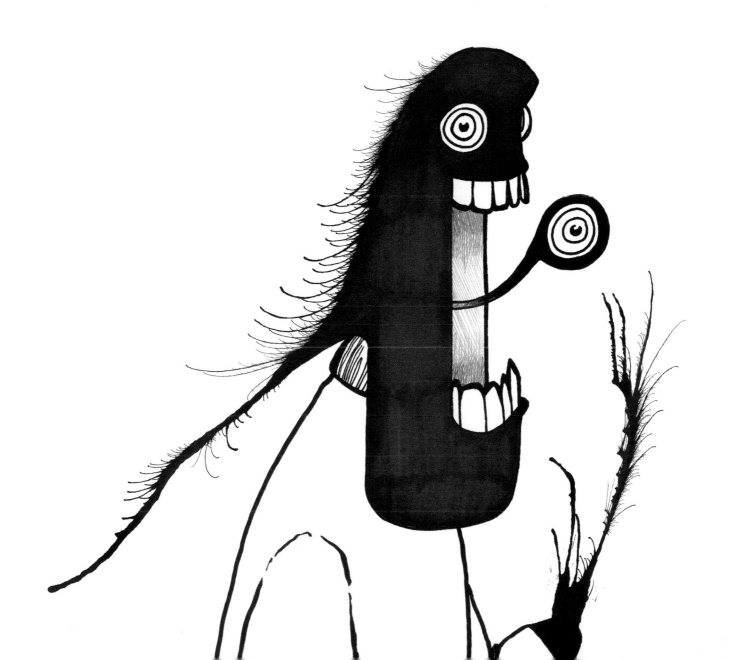

54

Halitosium Rex, or Hal for short, can stand completely still for hours waiting for the right tasty morsel to come along. His breath smells of rotting carrion to attract flies. But he doesn't eat the flies. Patience serves him well, as he waits for the flies to lay eggs on his soft, porous tongue, where they hatch and become a delicious treat for Hal.

Hal lives only in Dade County, Florida, where the flies are juiciest. So why, you may ask, does he wear the scarf? The scarf is actually a clever disguise. Hal's only true predator is the Stinkus Americus Eatimus, so he disguises himself as a Canadian, which the Stinkus finds too polite for his taste.

By Jessica Madison | January 10, 2007 at 08:04 A.M.

Drawing:
Sunday, 07 Jan 2007, 01:45 A.M.
Drawing posted:
Wednesday, 10 Jan 2007, 01:33 A.M.

As it turns out, Regigard WAS allergic to Dimetapp.

By Jessica L. Beers | January 10, 2007 at 12:00 P.M.

It started out innocently enough. Peter picked a peck of purple pickles from his favorite Peruvian purveyor. What Peter didn't know was that one pickle in the pack was planted to something. He pulled at the purple pickle, pursed his puckered lips and pounded the table when his hard work was not rewarded. What he didn't realize was his purple prize was really the tongue of a Polish polka party monster, Petronela. He got his tongue stuck to the bottom of a pickle pan one day while perusing some strange Pyrrhic polka tunes he heard in a cucumber field. He was picked up by the tongue, placed in a pickle pack and popped into a pretty little peck basket. Peter rescued poor Petronela that day in the market, thankfully. Now Peter has his own personal polka performer whenever he pleads.

By Sam Berkes | January 10, 2007 at 08:44 P.M.

He is the nasopharyngeal plinth of the class.

He drifts from desk to desk, sniffing out his seat, earning sneers and blatant denunciations from the classmates. They stack upon him their quandaries and refer to him only with disdain. He is the holder of all classes. This doesn't bother him.

He breathes the higher air, and holds more of it. He is an air camel, engaged to life. He is breathing and living and he is the plinth of the class. He holds their shortcomings for them and the students know this but don't acknowledge it. They are chalk dust. They are floating debris and he breathes them and holds them. He is a mother, cradling until maturation.

He hugs the weight of the world in his snout. He cannot catch a cold. He protects himself from sneezing. The students know this but don't acknowledge it. He holds the dust but is careful. He is waiting until he cannot wait. He is the nasopharyngeal plinth of the class and he is the winter and the air and the pedestal of disdain. This doesn't bother him. He accepts his duties. He is the weight and the dust and the mother. He is the truth and the light and the holder of all classes. He is the reduction of the students and the keeper of secrets; he is the silly monster with the serious job. He must hold a cold and prevent a sneeze.

He must tissue the tears of the students
and protect them from

themselves.

Drawing:
Sunday, 07 Jan 2007, 09:22 P.M.
Drawing posted:
Thursday, 11 Jan 2007, 03:31 A.M.

By Brooke Nelson | January 11, 2007 at 11:57 A.M.

Far be it for me to know what the next big handbag style is going to be. I'm just the designer, not the trend forecast professional. Last year, to everyone's surprise, was the year of the Woolly-bag. Equipped with faux mammoth trunk handles the bag was cumbersome and hard to hold. A large cartoonish eye served as the clasp, and rubberized stiletto heel scuff busters lined the bottoms of the atrocious carryalls. First created as an accessory to the now tired UGG® footwear line, the Woolly-bag didn't catch on in U.S. markets until Paris Hilton was seen carrying one to a dinner party. Of course, all fifteen-year-old Paris wannabes just had to have one. The market was flooded with orders, and soon they were everywhere. eBay was brimming over with cheap knockoffs. And just as soon as it took off, the pesky pocketbook went kaput. It's amazing what people will buy, just to look hip.

By Sam Berkes | January 11, 2007 at 08:18 P.M.

56

Drawing:
Sunday, 07 Jan 2007, 09:35 P.M.
Drawing posted:
Friday, 12 Jan 2007, 01:11 A.M.

And now a word from our sponsor:

"Hi, I'm Jack Coosteau and I'm telling all of you
to come on down to *Jack Coosteau's Tadpole City.*
We have hundreds, thousands, no, millions
of these wonderful tadpoles just waiting for you.

Here at *Jack Coosteau's Tadpole City* we have everything to fill your tadpole needs.

Every make and model, every color and size,
every gender, every flavor of Tadpole can be found
today at *Jack Coosteau's Tadpole City.*

New models, used models, even models that
haven't left the designer's drawing board yet,
you'll find them all at *Jack Coosteau's Tadpole City.*

Do you need a tadpole that only swims up river?
Do you need a tadpole that can guard the house when you're gone?
Do you need a tadpole that can seat a family of four?
We have it, and more, at *Jack Coosteau's Tadpole City.*

So come on down today. Bring the family.
Timmy the tapdancing tadpole will be entertaining
the kids with two, that's right, two shows daily.

That's *Jack Coosteau's Tadpole City*
on the corner of Water St. and River Blvd.
That's *Jack Coosteau's Tadpole City*
for all your tadpole needs."

We return you now to your regularly
scheduled stories, already in progress.

By Bill Bibo Jr. | January 12, 2007 at 06:59 A.M.

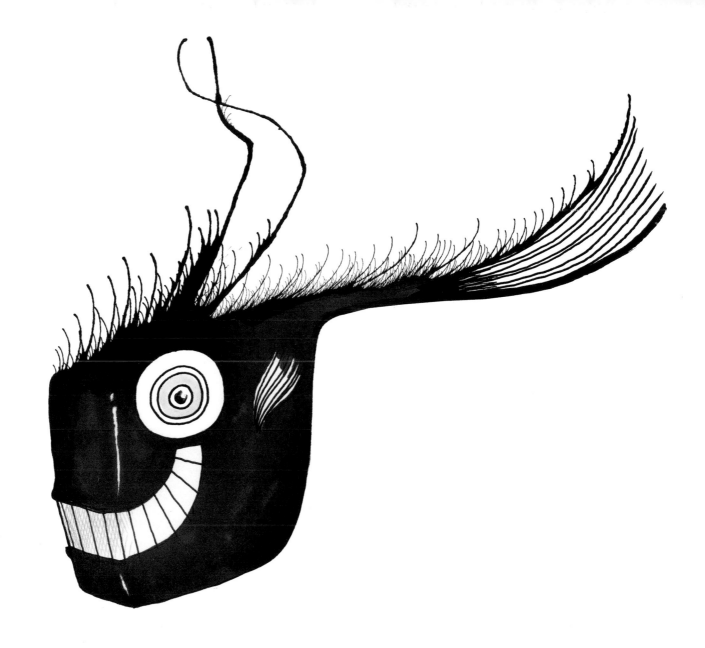

57

Drawing:
Sunday, 07 Jan 2007, 09:45 P.M.
Drawing posted:
Sunday, 07 Jan 2007, 04:00 A.M.

Orb was so excited to see FIVE packages under the tree at Christmas! And then...

By Annie Nordmark | January 13, 2007 at 08:36 A.M.

He just can't decide between mandarin orange, orange with a subtle parquet pattern, aurora borealis orange, bengal tiger orange, or the word that rhymes with orange orange. So he wore them all.

By Victoria Koldewyn | January 13, 2007 at 10:46 P.M.

They were all lined up perfectly in front of him. Five pencils. Five perfectly sharpened pencils. Their lengths exactly the same. Their spacing so exact. He adjusted the piece of paper a bit to the right. Perfectly aligned with the desk's edge. Just like the other four sheets peeking out beneath it. He stared at his desk for five minutes. Just sitting there. At five after five, he was ready to go home. He stood up and pushed his chair underneath his desk, its five wheels facing the same direction.

He walked the five blocks back to his apartment, which was the fifth door on the right on the fifth floor. Closing the door, he slid the chain, turned the three deadbolts and clicked the lock on the knob. He walked the five feet to the bar and placed the items in his pockets into corresponding trays. Five, of course. Change in the first tray, bills in the second, keys in the third, a small multi-tool in the fourth and miscellaneous items in the fifth. There were no miscellaneous items today, so he tapped the tray with a finger five times. He rounded the bar and opened the fridge to grab one of five premade sandwiches and one of five glasses of water. He would replace them before going to bed for the evening. Making his way to the pentagon-shaped dinner table, he paused to turn the TV to Channel 5.

As he calmly dined, he noticed a small red stain on his cuff. He looked at the side of his sandwich and then he realized what it was. He set down his meal, took five sips of water and proceeded to the bathroom. The light was flipped on and he gazed at himself in the mirror, his five orange ties staring back at him. The water heated up quickly and he dabbed at the stain and worked at it with the soap until he was satisfied. Turning the water off he stood erect and a smile crossed his face, despite the second tie having flopped out over its neighbors. His five upper and five lower teeth gleaming in the light. Tomorrow, he would kill Number Five and his job would be done.

By Terry Tolleson | January 13, 2007 at 11:45 P.M.

58

Nigel began his life as a deep-ocean dweller. His streamlined body and multiple eyes were a perfect match for his environment. That is, until he developed the most unfortunate of Yog-soloc maladies...

he became both nearsighted and farsighted, in alternating eyes.

Lacking seagoing ophthalmologists in his region, Nigel was forced to have himself grafted onto a spare sailor's body he had lying around the house. But once he got on land he...

By Katy Whitman | January 14, 2007 at 09:10 A.M.

Drawing:
Sunday, 07 Jan 2007, 09:55 P.M.
Drawing posted:
Sunday, 14 Jan 2007, 01:08 A.M.

But once he got on land he... had a harder time maneuvering the borrowed body. The knees buckled. The arms flapped. The tiny neck bent all four ways. What to do?

Nigel loped from the pier to a quiet alley and leaned against an old green Dumpster to think. Fish guts, McBacon sandwich wrappers, coat hangers, shredded tax returns and an old Xmas tree waited for Tuesday pickup while Nigel waited for an idea. When it came, ten eyes gleamed with excitement, two with pride.

He emerged from the alley, stiff limbed and head held high as he approached a lady eating her lunch on a bench. "Excuse me..." but he never got to ask his question for she started screaming quite loudly in his face. It was then he looked down to discover the bits of wire and tree limb sticking out of the flesh where he had poked them through to secure the joints. He made a mental note to trim them at his next stop, which was...

By Emily Reed | January 14, 2007 at 11:13 P.M.

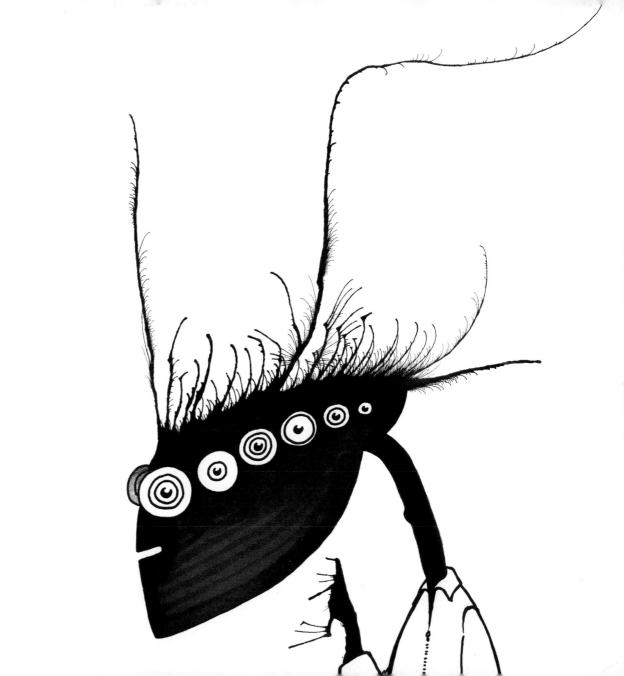

This monster is no joke. You may find his spines delightful, but they are a momentary diversion, a ruse to keep you from paying attention to that hungry maw, which will devour you, no mistake.

This is Demonicus Insatiable, the monster that is hungry for all things. Yes, his mouth has those delicate filters, which sift away the larger, unpalatable bits. But for all that, he is voracious. You have seen him at work across the dinner table; you have seen him on television; you see him in the mirror. He waits in the pit, ready to swallow whatever you release: desire, sorrow, anger, compassion. He does not discriminate. You let it go; it is his.

By Juliet Williams | January 15, 2007 at 09:33 P.M.

Drawing:
Sunday, 07 Jan 2007, 10:17 P.M.
Drawing posted:
Monday, 15 Jan 2007, 12:05 A.M.

59:

MAAARGHYAHHHHRGGGGHHH HYAAAAAABOOOORRGGGHHHHH!

off-page:
Do you want fries with that?

By Yi Shun Lai | January 16, 2007 at 12:03 P.M.

Fishing tackle in the eye really hurts.
Makes the hair on the back of your neck stand up.

By Jessica L. Beers | January 29, 2007 at 10:29 A.M.

60

Having settled for a dead-end, boring accounting job just after college with the smallest accounting firm in the city, Clayton Bartleby desperately needs a creative outlet. Searching for months in vain for the outlet to express his pent-up emotions, Clayton gives up in despair. The very next night Clayton finds himself in a bad part of town, having flown off course in one of the updrafts that the city tends to create. It's a part of the city he has never seen before. Thirsty, he wanders into a nearby club, where he discovers his dream of dreams, his purpose in this present life. Now after years of devotion to his newfound craft, Mr. Clayton Bartleby can be found most nights headlining at the Tooky Tiki club as their resident cancan-dancing, flying marionette puppet master! Yay for Clay!

By Jake McTyre | January 16, 2007 at 06:54 A.M.

Drawing:
Sunday, 07 Jan 2007, 10:22 P.M.
Drawing posted:
Tuesday, 16 Jan 2007, 02:08 A.M.

Dookie knew he'd never be a match for a late, great blonde bombshell. But when he spotted a certain iconic subway grate on Fifty-second and Lex, he just had to give it a go.

By Yi Shun Lai | January 16, 2007 at 12:40 P.M.

As he took his bow on this fateful evening, he realized that his dorsal tentacles were not behaving! They disliked the role of posing as lowly "marionette strings" and had been vying for a larger role for some time now. They had been happy in Clay's old life of accounting, for they gave Clay an advantage when it came to entering figures into the computer (they are very agile)! Clay tried to distract them by launching into a encore cancan performance, but as he watched in horror, the tentacles reached for his fellow marionettes on stage and…

By Katy Whitman | January 16, 2007 at 01:08 P.M.

…tickled them. The tentacles tickled the fellow marionettes so violently that they fell to the floor in roaring laughter. The puppet master was so furious with this display of unprofessional behavior that he gave Clayton the starring role in the cancan performance (along with national exposure in all their advertising campaigns) and punished the other lowly, giggling marionettes by…

By Amy Fedele | January 16, 2007 at 01:42 P.M.

…tangling up their strings like a big tangled thing, so that none of them could prance and pronate. Undeterred, the marionettes presented the knotty situation (their bums and bits were bumping together!) to Clayton, who in addition to being a former accountant with massive dexterity, was also a Junior Monster Scout and had won numerous badges for tying, retying and untying undying and un-ending variations of knots known to man, cancan dancer and monster alike.

By Victoria Koldewyn | January 16, 2007 at 10:11 P.M.

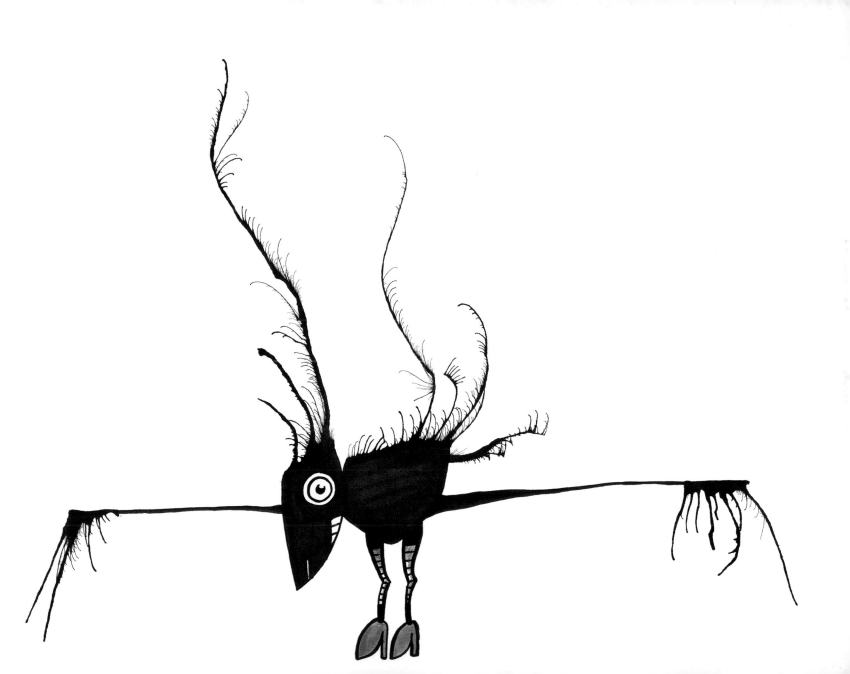

61

Six o'clock rolled around and sure enough, in stepped Tomas through the imitation leather sway door. Some people in the karaoke bar acknowledged his presence with a nod. The DJ gave a half-hearted look in his direction and pulled out the overused track that would see yet another night of butchery. He sat at a nondescript table and a waitress dropped a glass of the bar's stoutest "drink" available. Tomas threw it back and winced a little as the heavy liquor oozed down his throat. Three guests finished their renditions of their favorite tunes and Tomas gleefully sauntered to the stage. This was his time to shine. It never mattered how everyone else heard him—never. He was just keen on getting up there and belting it out.

The notes rattled out of Tomas's mouth while his tongue wagged the ephemeral keys. He hit a couple of notes at such a pitch that no one could have possibly heard anything. Oh, but they did. This went on for about two minutes worth of the song and then it happened. The first head tilted back lazily. Then, suddenly, and all at once, everyone in the bar fell into a peculiar slumber. Tomas hopped off the stage, continuing to sing, and began rifling through pockets, purses, registers, anything that might hold valuables. He got his satisfaction, all the while joyfully singing along with the speakers, hopped back up on stage and did a few more verses. Everyone seemed to come to without appearing disoriented or otherwise knowledgeable that any time had passed while unconscious. The song concluded and Tomas stepped off the stage, his jacket a little puffier than before.

By Terry Tolleson | January 17, 2007 at 03:21 P.M.
Read the expanded version of this story on the DVD

Drawing:
Sunday, 07 Jan 2007, 10:45 P.M.
Drawing posted:
Wednesday, 17 Jan 2007, 02:44 A.M.

Ahhhhh! Nooooo! Not Windows XP— and not that @#@$! Office Assistant paperclip!!

Thus spoke Zarafoostruh, clerk and go-fetch boy. At least he doesn't do that awful wispy comb-over thing.

By Victoria Koldewyn | January 17, 2007 at 11:47 P.M.

Svensen yelped in embarrassment as his toupee flew off before the entire office awaiting his presentation on *Brine & Its Effects on the Seaconomy.*

By Jessica L. Beers | January 29, 2007 at 10:33 A.M.

It's the same story we've heard hundreds of times before. Boy takes tour of candy plant. Boy spills barrel of toxic refuse. Toxic refuse spills into copper candy kettle. End result:

radioactive mutant spice drops.

Spice drops are usually seen as docile and sweet. Mutant spice drops, however, are quite different. Complete with sugar tendrils and rocky choppers, these little bastards are tough. Their pectin hearts burn with furious molten sugary fervor. They can blind you from ten feet away with razor-sharp granulated sugar spit wads.

By Sam Berkes | January 18, 2007 at 08:28 P.M.
Read the expanded version of this story on the DVD

This monster is Snarkus McFarley, former manager of Chainsaws R Us in Ebbettsville, Indiana. Snarkus was actually a human being back when he worked at Chainsaws R Us. But one fateful day, an angry customer stormed into the shop, shouting that the chain on his brand-new chainsaw had, once again, fallen off. Enormously frustrated without his chainsaw to use as an outlet for his anger, this furious customer seized Snarkus by his head and pulled it clean off. I suppose I should not say "clean," because it was a messy incident. Blood, veins, arteries, etc. trailed from Snarkus's head. Using his veins and arteries as appendages, he scooched himself to the Ebbettsville River where he began his life as a freshwater monster squid.

By Juliet Williams | January 18, 2007 at 09:13 P.M.
Read the expanded version of this story on the DVD

Drawing:
Sunday, 07 Jan 2007, 10:55 P.M.
Drawing posted:
Thursday, 18 Jan 2007, 04:30 A.M.

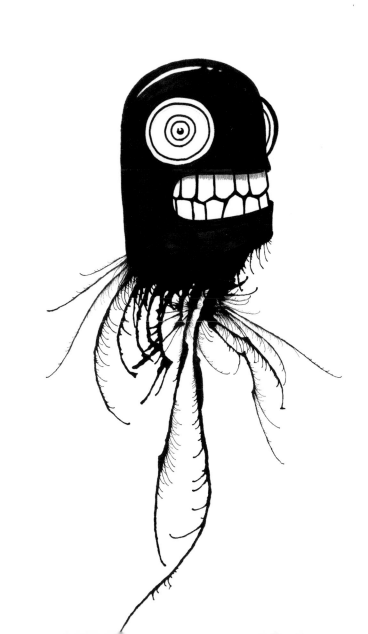

Monster 63 is not any normal monster. Monster 63 is also Inspector #128!
Yes, the Prodigy that is Inspector #128, the most revered and sought-after
sock and stocking inspector in the entire town! He's virtually a celebrity.
He can diagnose a bad sock or stocking from one hundred yards. This gift,
this blessing to all monsterkind, is not the only thing he can and does brag
about, though. He also has a championship-winning mustache that he uses
to spin plates with. Ah, Monster #63 (or 190, as his friends might call him),
your exploits and talents will be sung of for days after you're gone!

By Jake McTyre | January 19, 2007 at 07:15 A.M.

Drawing:
Sunday, 07 Jan 2007, 11:11 P.M.
Drawing posted:
Friday, 19 Jan 2007, 03:42 A.M.

This guy is one of the greatest unsolved X-files that never aired.
The deadly Ringed Sock Worm of Bangor, Maine, has terrorized
the state for over two centuries.

Characterized by a unipodal body, thick stringy facial antennae,
full protective body sock and large peepers, it's fairly easy
to pick out of a crowd.

Only attacking in the dead of night, the Ringed Sock Worm seduces its prey with hypnotic circular patterns created in its outer skin.

Once the victim is under its spell, the Sock Worm hugs its victim
to death in a cozy strangle hold. Dinner is served.

To date, about 137 deaths have been confirmed, but 204 additional
victims are currently unidentified. The Bangor police department
is working hard to keep this creature at bay.

By Sam Berkes | January 19, 2007 at 11:50 P.M.

Merflin revved her engine and prepared
to take first in the Worm Race 2095.

By Jessica L. Beers | January 29, 2007 at 11:16 A.M.

64

Too many stamps,
too many envelopes.
That's how you get
the big, big tongue,
the blue tongue of bleah.

Oh yeah, oh yeah.
The blue tongue of bleah.
Oh yeah, oh yeah.

By Juliet Williams | January 20, 2007 at 04:40 P.M.

The trouble with invisible steel poles is that you can't see them on cold winter days,

so if you happen to feel like walking around with your tongue
hanging out for no reason at all, you could very likely get stuck
to one and be there for a very long time. Tragic really.
We'll just have to wait for spring to come and thaw him out.

By Sabeyen Daila | January 20, 2007 at 07:48 P.M.

What he had initially thought to be the Noro Virus turned out to be
something more... there was a light growing inside of him...

By Jessica L. Beers | January 29, 2007 at 11:32 A.M.

Drawing:
Sunday, 07 Jan 2007, 11:30 P.M.
Drawing posted:
Saturday, 20 Jan 2007, 12:59 A.M.

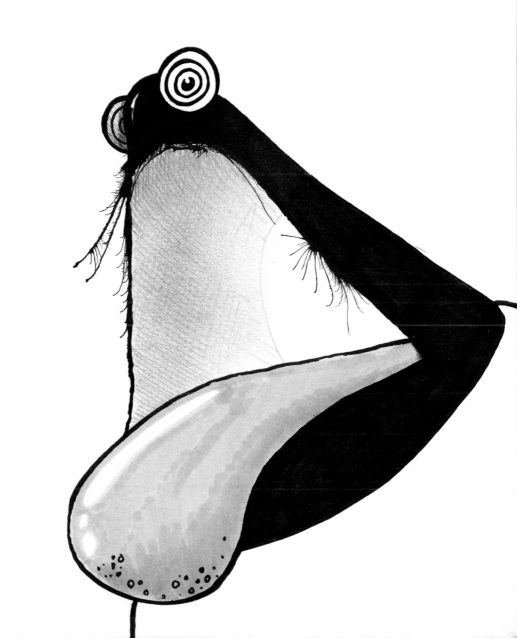

Number 65 is obviously a pygmy pigment monster. Ink tanks are injected with these microscopic pygmies to promote better quality and output. They come in two flavors: waterproof for traditional inkjet printers and extra dry for toner cartridges. It seems your pygmy monsters are acting up, Stefan. They too are smarmy little devils that require lots of attention and care. Hopefully they start acting like normal for your Monday deadlines. If not, I know they respond well to hard jolts and bumps. Give the printer a nice whack on the side to set 'em straight, it works every time.

By Sam Berkes | January 21, 2007 at 05:07 P.M.

Drawing:
Sunday, 07 Jan 2007, 11:35 P.M.
Drawing posted:
Sunday, 07 Jan 2007, 04:00 A.M.

It was the annual talent show, and everyone knew what was coming.

"Hey, guys! Look at me! Look at me! I'm Jay Leno!"

Sheesh, Dexter *always* did Jay Leno.
Sure, the resemblance was uncanny, but c'mon, they thought, for once can't you do your M. Night Shyamalan?

By Pimpom Tomlinson | January 21, 2007 at 06:13 P.M.

Yes, yes, YESSSS! This is the BEST superball prize I ever got from the gumball machine! It's personalized: I tell it to bounce, and it asks me, "How high?" I tell it I want it to leave bounce-prints all over my big brother's favorite Twisted Sister T-shirt personally signed by Dee Snider and it asks, "How many? Any specific pattern? Or areas in particular you want me to cover up?" It's the best two-bit piece I've spent in years!

By Victoria Koldewyn | January 21, 2007 at 09:38 P.M.

Today is the happiest day of Gary's life to date.
He has just begun to sprout.

By Jessica L. Beers | January 29, 2007 at 11:37 A.M.

66

Drawing:
Sunday, 07 Jan 2007, 11:43 P.M.
Drawing posted:
Monday, 22 Jan 2007, 03:57 A.M.

The illusive Bill Proudmane was once proud of his exquisite mane of long, fine, flowing locks. Unfortunately, male-pattern baldness hit him at an early age. However, not one to stay down (and always having an ace up his sleeve), he now waxes the place where hair appears no more.

Bill is one of those troublemakers that you would never suspect is a troublemaker. The kind that, if you would see him walking down the street, you would think to yourself, "There goes a nice fellow. Probably not very interesting, though." However, Bill has a rather interesting habit of using his large reflective surface, which now sits where hair once sat to shine the sun into the eyes of unsuspecting souls just going about their daily business.

You can tell he's rather chipper at the moment, posing for the camera and giving a thumbs up, his tail proudly outward in a stance that tells leaps and bounds of self-achievement. Obviously he's just shone some unsuspecting individual when they were least expecting it.

Should you ever find yourself driving along, and off to one side there's a rather bright glare off of someone's windshield... more likely than not, that's just Bill, doing what he does best.

So next time this happens to you, don't get annoyed. Just chuckle to yourself and go, "Oh, that Bill. He's got a nice set of neck rings."

By Matt Latzke | January 22, 2007 at 07:41 A.M.

Leron Camron was the inspiration for the disastrous dirigible created by the late Count Ferdinand von Zeppelin. His massive snout was gravitationally impervious and Zeppelin wondered how it was possible. It turns out our friend Leron had quite a dangerous hydrogen-sniffing habit. Zeppelin took this and ran with it, creating the first flying hydrogen bomb.

By Sam Berkes | January 22, 2007 at 10:58 P.M.

Septha was shocked and saddened by the speed and closeness with which the spaceship had passed him by. They had slowed down just enough to make him think they were going to give him a ride before swerving and accelerating past him at a frightening proximity. "How will I ever make it to Dafne's on time?"

By Jessica L. Beers | January 29, 2007 at 11:49 A.M.

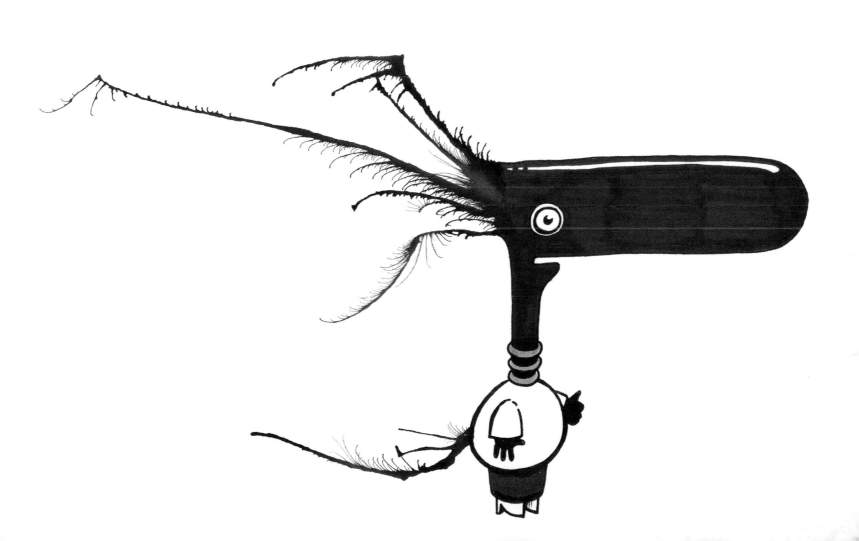

67

Drawing:
Sunday, 07 Jan 2007, 11:50 P.M.
Drawing posted:
Tuesday, 23 Jan 2007, 03:06 A.M.

As an opera virtuoso, Nigel left much to be desired. But he had such lofty aspirations as a young pod! His devotion to the art had been insatiable. He practiced incessantly— for his mother had always told him that "practice makes perfect!"

He practiced so much that he could not keep a roommate, his landlords canceled his leases because of noise complaints and after years of having to house her own aging son, his own mother told him to "Give it a rest, why don't you?!" With that he tried to stop, for he always listened to his mother... but much to his dismay, his mother was right once again... She had always said, "If you keep making that face it will freeze that way." And much to Nigel's horror—it had. (Now what does he do with himself?)

By Katy Whitman | January 23, 2007 at 05:58 A.M.

A sophisticated being, James was most proud of two things: First being his extensive knowledge and appreciation of expressionist paintings, second being his perfectly groomed mustache.

Unfortunately for him, one fateful December morning, after learning that Edvard Munch's The Scream was damaged beyond repair, James too screamed. He has since stayed in this position. Some say he just snapped. Others say it's in honor of The Scream. Some just say he likes to show off how long he can stay in one position.

By Matt Latzke | January 23, 2007 at 12:28 P.M.

Paxil tab meets The Scream and sings *Fiddler on the Roof.*

By Owen W. Swain | January 23, 2007 at 05:20 P.M.

The last thing he remembers from his eighth-grade shop class is someone shouting, "Seymour, look out for that vise!"

By Juliet Williams | January 23, 2007 at 08:50 P.M.

68

Drawing:
Monday, 08 Jan 2007, 12:00 A.M.
Drawing posted:
Wednesday, 24 Jan 2007, 05:11 A.M.

This is the "after" picture.
Before he was 38,976,000 tons,
and him shirtless was not a pleasant sight *at all*.
Thank heavens for Atkins.

By **Sabeyen Daila** | January 24, 2007 at 03:58 P.M.

Happy shirtless goat,
Bug-eyed, white nippled; so haute.
His name is Carl.

By **Sam Berkes** | January 24, 2007 at 09:59 P.M.

YESSSS! It's the peri-annual Monster Love-In Fest!
Grab your favorite Pez, a blanket and some baby grub oil—
last one with your shirt on is a party pooper.

By **Victoria Koldewyn** | January 24, 2007 at 10:44 P.M.

"Gah, man—that ride was totally wicked!"
breathed Svector, still reeling
from the rambunctious tenacity
of the Spincthelkser.

By **Jessica L. Beers** | January 29, 2007 at 12:09 P.M.

He's grumpy because you drew him sitting on a branch. "Why is it always the branch?" he wonders. "Why are birds always drawn on branches?!" Do they ever draw birds somewhere interesting? No! You never see a cartoon bird at a nightclub, or in a rollercoaster car. Only on that boring old branch. Clearly you need to get over your prejudiced image of birds, and beg him for forgiveness.

By **Sabeyen Daila** | January 25, 2007 at 03:59 P.M.

69 BOOM!

Drawing:
Wednesday, 24 Jan 2007, 02:45 A.M.
Drawing posted:
Thursday, 25 Jan 2007, 06:47 A.M.

The morning sun had hit Fisher almost as hard as an invisible wall. BOOM! The noise was deafening. BOOM! BOOM! Wait, thought Fisher, the sun made no sound. BOOM! In the field stood a couple of the two-leggers and they had sticks that made the terrible BOOM! He watched as they pointed their sticks in the sky and made the terrible noise that hurt his early morning head. BOOM! BOOM! One of the two-leggers threw his stick to the ground in anger and stomped off in the direction of his square nest. The other followed.

The early bird gets the worm, his mother had told him, so he flew to where the two-leggers had stood. The stick was still there where the one had thrown it. All around the stick were strange straight worms. They all had shells unlike normal worms. Fisher found one with a long, pointed head. He grabbed it and flew back to his tree.

The worm has hard, almost as hard as a stone. Fisher's stomach rumbled. Last night's drinking had made him hungry. With such a hard shell the meat of the worm must be very tender, thought Fisher salivating slightly, and he bit down with all his hungover might.

The explosion shook all the leaves from his branch but one. When Fisher was able to pry his claws from the branch and fly away he vowed never again to eat fermented berries, and never again to eat early morning worms. Especially if they had a shell.

By **Bill Bibo Jr.** | January 25, 2007 at 08:42 P.M.
Read the expanded version of this story on the DVD

Helsinki crackled and crisped, the shock still ringing in his ears.
"Leaf on an open power line... very clever, Vanderblart... very clever."

By **Jessica L. Beers** | January 29, 2007 at 12:18 P.M.

Drawing:
Wednesday, 24 Jan 2007, 02:55 A.M.
Drawing posted:
Thursday, 26 Jan 2007, 06:47 A.M.

Larry felt that he was looking quite sharp with his pinstripe pants and suit coat. Obviously he is in a fine mood, about to go teach his philosophy course at the local community college. The real question that we have for Larry is, how do you fit your sporty yellow shirt on over your rather large cranium?

One theory is that Larry does not actually have a body like the one pictured at all... and that he's simply in his natural habitat—inside a mannequin at your local clothing store. How tricky!

By Matt Latzke | January 26, 2007 at 11:29 A.M.

This particular monster is an Eatus Yurheadus,

a very rare monster indeed. As his name would suggest, Monster 70 eats heads, being that he is mostly just a head himself. He then attaches himself to his prey's body with his long, rubbery tail. And in this way, Monster 70 can do all the things he's always wanted to do. Like wearing polyester and going to disco parties.

By Sabeyen Daila | January 26, 2007 at 12:38 P.M.

Dear Boss,

I am not a Suit. Please fire me. I haven't the strength to quit. I cannot type another memo. I cannot answer another phone. I cannot conference call or inventory, or balance, or alphabetize again. Please fire me.
I am a monster within a Suit.

Sincerely,
#70

By Brooke Nelson | January 26, 2007 at 03:17 P.M.

"Yeeesssss??" slithered Phlan,
eager to please on his first day on the lot.

By Jessica L. Beers | January 29, 2007 at 12:28 P.M.

A drop descended from the syringe and fell into the fluid below with a delicate splash. It bubbled slightly, then began to churn a bit more violently, until finally a hardy head of foam grew to the edge of the beaker. It radiated red and yellow and orange and white. Tongs were used to grip the container and pour it into a cast-iron funnel. The newly viscous concoction coated the sides as it crawled into the awaiting chamber. Once finished, the lid was screwed on tight. A few clicks of buttons introduced life to an inanimate object. Nioldul Fisk removed his goggles and gloves, all the while smiling at the product of his many labors through late nights.

Everything seemed to be in working order. "This will make them understand my intelligence, my contributions to this institution. My being under-appreciated will go on no longer!" He straightened his white coat, as immaculate as the room in which he worked, before carefully setting the mechanism on a low-lying, wheeled cart. Fisk placed a steel cover over the machine and cart. His mouth opened with gleeful laughter, baring his lower teeth, as he levitated across the room. The name badge on his coat was relatively small, and that had always bothered Fisk. "They will certainly know my name after today." He spun around to escort the cart to one of the more populated lecture halls at the university.

The class stirred only occasionally throughout the professor's review. The students seemed to be even more lethargic and unemotional than normal. This particular lecture must have been dreadfully boring.

By Terry Tolleson | January 27, 2007 at 01:56 A.M.
Read the expanded version of this story on the DVD

And then entered Nioldul Fisk,

slamming through the doors with his cart leading the way. Gasps were heard in a giant wave up the rows of the room. The professor turned sharply to face Fisk. "What is the meaning of this?!" he barked. Fisk simply ignored the pompous windbag and threw off the cover hiding his invention. "This will fix everything! You all will thank me and this school will finally give Nioldul Fisk his due!" He flipped a switch, and the device hummed brilliantly before the crowd. Within moments the room became warm; quite warm. Only a few seconds had passed and the room was at a very comfortable degree.

The auditorium had been dreadfully cold, on account of the broken heating system, a result of the freeze over the past few nights. As the Senior Facilities Engineer (the fancy name the university gave its custodial staff), Fisk decided to make an extremely effective heater. And effective it was. And appreciated it was. Affirmed only by the students, of course.

"Fisk, lad," queried the professor, "what did you say was the name of the creator of this exquisite device?" After recovering from the shock, Fisk sternly stared while his mustache bristled and pointed at a little plaque on the side of the heater. And the professor read: "Yet Another Nioldul Fisk Creation" as Fisk stomped out of the room.

72

Drawing:
Wednesday, 24 Jan 2007, 03:15 A.M.
Drawing posted:
Saturday, 28 Jan 2007, 06:05 A.M.

This is DJ Jarred Jumpsalot, host of the popular Rock 'em Songs for the Kids on 96.4 KQXE FM. DJ Jarred is a hip dude who digs the rock 'n' roll, especially the old school tunes from groups like Ike & Tina, the Spinners and classics like Dion's "Runaround Sue." His tagline is "Hey, dig it."

When he broadcasts from remote locations, the kids flock to his Monster Van and plead for autographs and for him to do his patented DJ Jarred Jump. What you see here is one fan's rendering of DJ Jarred's Jump outside of Freddie the Mattress King's showroom on March 27, 2005.

By Juliet Williams | January 28, 2007 at 06:13 P.M.

Hello ma baby, hello ma honey, hello ma ragtime gal. Words synonymous with a famously persnickety froggy, Michigan J. Few people know about Michigan's big brother, Indiana I. He doesn't usually seek the limelight, so this rare glimpse of promenade is quite superb. He usually just sits around his house watching the Food Network, snacking on whatever he can get his hands on. So to see him actually jumping around is a sight.

By Sam Berkes | January 28, 2007 at 08:19 P.M.

When Gaston was a kid, his mother would sing to him and his four siblings,

"Five little monsters jumping on the bed one fell off and broke his head..."

Which is really the original song; there were no monkeys.
They evolved after the Monsters and falsely copywrote it as their own (cheeky mammalia that they are).

Despite his mother's good advice and the demise of his other brothers and sisters, Gaston survives to this day. He learned from Daisy, Gerald, Moulin and Claire's bad jumping mistakes, developed his own techniques and now makes a living as an acrobat in Cirque du Soleil. And he still jumps on the bed.

By Victoria Koldewyn | January 29, 2007 at 12:09 A.M.

73

Ahhh… the mating dance of the majestic rare Red-heeled Spring-back.
Notice how the subtle bobbing of the head calls attention to its beautiful plumage.
Whether this male will be successful in his endeavor will depend
upon the frequency and depth of his bobbing torso. Will he be successful?
We will have to watch…

By Katy Whitman | January 29, 2007 at 08:49 A.M.

Drawing:
Wednesday, 24 Jan 2007, 03:25 A.M.
Drawing posted:
Monday, 29 Jan 2007, 04:56 A.M.

I gots me a neck as long as a snorkel—
I gots me a neck. Can you guess what it's there for?
I gots me a neck. Bobs me head up and down—
I gots me a neck. At the end, never a frown.

I gots me four legs, and I'll give you a hint:
Legs and neck, they do the same thing.
You guessed ever so right. I can see it in your eyes.
You guessed these appendages serve to make me so fly.

I'm the hip-hoppin'
Beat-boxin'
Monster of the Day

By Yi Shun Lai | January 29, 2007 at 03:30 P.M.
Read the expanded version of this story on the DVD

Through the course of evolution, this magnificent species has manifested the strange effect
of their rubber-fruit fetish. They were already gifted with flexibility, and now with the
characteristics of rubber, they have uncontrollable movement of their joints. Try as they might,
but their increased calcium intake has done little to help. Maybe this mutation is a blessing,
but as they attempt to maneuver through the dense forest, the numerous bumps
on their heads do not think so.

By Danielle Ngo | January 29, 2007 at 03:48 P.M.

Janella's neck extension got a little out of hand at the chiropractor
but she subsequently ate her health professional for lunch
and is satisfied the score has been evened.

By Owen W. Swain | January 29, 2007 at 06:59 P.M.

74

Drawing:
Wednesday, 24 Jan 2007, 03:30 A.M.
Drawing posted:
Tuesday, 30 Jan 2007, 04:15 A.M.

They reached the summit in good time. Hito looked back at his son, Tetsuo, and lent him a hand to pull him the rest of the way up. They gazed out over the horizon, down into the valley to see the tiny village below. The Fukei River seemed but a miniscule blue serpent tracking through the valley. Forests, lush with vegetation, grew healthy in the east while the Lesser Tonju Peek stared at them from the north. Just beyond was an enormous structure that slowly bobbed and dipped.

"The Great Mantalius guides us well today, my son." For centuries, his village had found a home on the back of the Great Mantalius and had developed an almost symbiotic relationship with the gargantuan beast. From this height, Tetsuo could peer down the mountain and see the many legs of the creature pacing through the plains.

It was starting to get late. Hito stood up and packed everything away. "The wings will be closing soon, we should make our way back to the village." They took once last, tranquil look at the outside world and as they headed down the mountainside, the Great Mantalius bent its head to look behind at the climbers. It gave a chortling sound and resumed its journey while the wings started to close overhead.

"It saw us, Father. That's good luck, right?"
"It's a blessing, Tetsuo. A god has spoken with us."

By Terry Tolleson | January 30, 2007 at 10:29 P.M.
Read the expanded version of this story on the DVD

"I don't understand," David stated, turning to look at the group of lab-coated people standing with him in the hallway. "What was so important?" "Well, we have never seen anything like this," offered a senior scientist stepping out from the group. "We have set up x-ray emitters in the room," he explained, pulling a small remote from his lab coat. A click. Something strange happened.

The creature changed. The large bulb on its back, which had been solid black, became crystal clear.

David stared in amazement; inside he could see land.

A minuscule mountain range sat inside the now translucent bubble. A forest with trees colored in summer green foliage could be seen, as well as what appeared to be a small city tucked in the back. David just stared. Then he could see them; along the side where the bubble ended, he could just barely see them. Tiny little black people, a perfect likeness of humanity only a millimeter tall gazing back at him. David was transfixed. "That's interesting ... "

Then the creature moved. It had turned its neck to stare back at David. "Very interesting," the creature spoke. Then it returned its attention back to the corner and began, slowly, to waft.

By Emmo Gates | January 30, 2007 at 11:41 P.M.
Read the expanded version of this story on the DVD

75

Doctor Postulatory, pre-eminent ornithologist of the Upper Realm, had been searching for

the elusive Pelican-Beaked Frazzletop

for years now. He knew only that the bird was a critical factor in the fertilization
of the endangered Frondy-Frilled Bulbous Spider Lily.

Now, staring at the curious specimen bobbing happily if somewhat confusedly
along the cobblestone road of Piccadilly Circus, he suddenly realized
that perhaps he just hadn't dug far enough in his studies of the plant...

By **Yi Shun Lai** | January 31, 2007 at 12:45 P.M.

Once upon a time there was a monster in the woods.
This monster went to the fire-breathing dinosaur dragon land
and he had a race with them. He won and did a silly monster dance.

By **William Hunt, age 5** | January 31, 2007 at 04:05 P.M.

Swaying to and fro, the Colossal-beak Farron sleeps high above the ground.
This majestic fowl has such great balance, even the highest winds can't knock it off
of its perch. Circular patterns in the shape of eyes are positioned atop its head
to ward off predators while slumbering. This feature is useful to the Farron as it sleeps
for up to twenty-two hours straight. They only eat once a day, usually between
3:30 and 3:44 in the morning, but even a small amount of sustenance will provide them
with enough energy to survive in the wild.

By **Sam Berkes** | January 31, 2007 at 08:26 P.M.

Everyone knows that before swivel-hipped hula girls on dashboards
of Monte Carlos, there were swivel-legged Frizzles riding the rough-hewn
handlebars of vintage Schwinns.

Well, if you didn't know that before, you do now! And don't you wish you had one?

By **Victoria Koldewyn** | January 31, 2007 at 10:52 P.M.

76

Bob lost his legs in a tragic accident that had three beneficial side effects: He grew chin hair, learned to fly and developed an amazing singing voice. He is now heard belting it out, like his idol Frank, in clubs across the western seaboard. He brings a whole new meaning to the term lounge lizard.

By Owen W. Swain | February 01, 2007 at 09:45 A.M.

Drawing:
Wednesday, 31 Jan 2007, 12:50 A.M.
Drawing posted:
Thursday, 01 Feb 2007, 04:43 A.M.

76 does not *hover,* you silly man! He's supported by invisible wire!

We're not sure WHY he was cast as Peter Pan at our local theater (after all, he has a beard and sings bass) but cast he was.

He's still not quite used to the flying, though. As you can tell by his face, he's doing his best to hide his fear of heights from the audience... doesn't seem to be working too well...

By Sabeyen Daila | February 01, 2007 at 04:43 P.M.

Keon Velocious is team captain of the Monstrock Stars, pre-eminent Hover Derby champions of the planet. And with the Hoverjam 2050 Derby Series finale fast approaching, the team was working hard to keep on top of their game. Practice was moving along smoothly, and the Stars were shining bright. Nothing pleased Keon more than to see a beautifully executed hover-check or a two-monster catch 'n' throw performed to exact standard in the practice ring.

By Sam Berkes | February 01, 2007 at 07:51 P.M.

77

Drawing:
Wednesday, 31 Jan 2007, 01:10 A.M.
Drawing posted:
Friday, 02 Feb 2007, 04:50 A.M.

Coy Roy's been redeployed to Fun-tyme Toys of Illinois. He's supposed to be overjoyed, but he's mostly just annoyed. Being an errand boy among the hoi polloi in a factory of toys is just not enough for Roy. He has tasted Hawaiian poi, enjoys a nice cold LaCroix and simply loves a good bok choy. He quit the toys and is currently unemployed, out to find the real McCoy, a day job as ball boy for the White Sox of Illinois.

By Sam Berkes
February 02, 2007 at 07:38 P.M.

For the longest time, Glen just sat there. Staring at his computer. Like it would tell him what to do. It wasn't even turned on. The office was unusually quiet. That's not accurate. Seven months ago, that statement would have meant something. Now, however, it was quite usual for there to be no sounds. Now the only one there was Glen. There was no power, so the soft sound of humming computers was absent as well. For the last seven months, Glen was all alone. And he had no idea why. He simply continued his routine, day in, day out. Trudging home after a day of nothing at the office. Checking the perpetually empty mailbox. Flipping the switch on the TV that wouldn't turn on. For the last seven months, not a single soul to interact with. Just Glen and his own thoughts. He slumped into his couch, finding it difficult to hold his eyes open. There were people eight months ago to interact with.

Not anymore.
Nothing.

Glen was being wheeled down to the new radiological lab for some experimental therapy. Lights passed overhead as his bed was pushed past other patient rooms and nurse stations. Glen lay motionless without exhibiting any reaction as the blinding fluorescence crossed his face.

By Terry Tolleson | February 02, 2007 at 09:41 P.M.
Read the expanded version of this story on the DVD

"Are you sure this will work, doctor?" questioned the nurse pushing the gurney. The doctor reviewed a chart, "This radiation treatment might just break his coma. The new lab is pretty much a bomb shelter, though, with the amount of radiation they'll hit Mr. Darton with." The nurse looked down at Glen. "What do you think's been going through his mind these last two years?" "Who knows, really? We just keep talking to them and interacting as best we can in hopes they'll respond to some form of stimulus. They say coma patients can hear us."

Once inside the lap, they strapped Glen under a large machine that looked like two large slabs of metal, with Glen sandwiched between them. The physicians exited the lab to proceed to the control room. Once the lab was sealed, a large commotion came from one of the nurse stations. People started gasping and becoming alarmed as they stared at a TV mounted to the wall. Seeing a small flash out of the corner of his eye, the doctor turned to face the window. The ensuing shockwave spread across the landscape at breakneck speed. Within mere moments the entirety of the hospital was engulfed in vaporizing death. All except the bomb-shelter-like lab. Nothing remained of the immense city but that solitary room. A room no one would find, as dust and debris would bury it for who knows how long. Well… at least seven months—and counting.

The thermal currents were strong today. Hermie was very happy.
He would glide for miles, dive low, swoop the top of buildings.
He narrowly missed a satellite dish he hadn't seen until almost too late.
He curved wide and high, returning to the spot where the thermal
currents were strongest.

Dare he try it today? It had been years since he had performed
the Filbert Maneuver. Today conditions were perfect. Go for it, he thought.

He gathered up speed and shot for the perfect draft of hot air. POW!
Straight up he flew, higher and higher and higher still. He curved,
he flipped, he somersaulted over a flock of startled geese.

Exhausted he landed on a nearby rooftop. Yes, flying conditions were
perfect and they should remain so for quite some time. There seemed
to be an endless supply of warm currents drifting up. Hermie knew
he would love living in Washington, DC.

By **Bill Bibo Jr.** | February 03, 2007 at 07:16 A.M.

Drawing:
Wednesday, 31 Jan 2007, 01:25 A.M.
Drawing posted:
Saturday, 03 Feb 2007, 12:42 A.M.

You know that little humming sound that's always in your ears?
Now we know what it is. It's the sound of

the Flying Dust Mite Brothers,

moving all around you, everywhere.

Just imagine if we could actually SEE them, too. What a sight
that would be. As many flying mites as the national debt gathered
all around you, no matter where you go.

Occasionally, you can feel one near your ear, or your nose,
or your eyelash. Try to keep from scratching;
it would be a shame to kill them.

By **Annie Nordmark** | February 03, 2007 at 07:47 A.M.

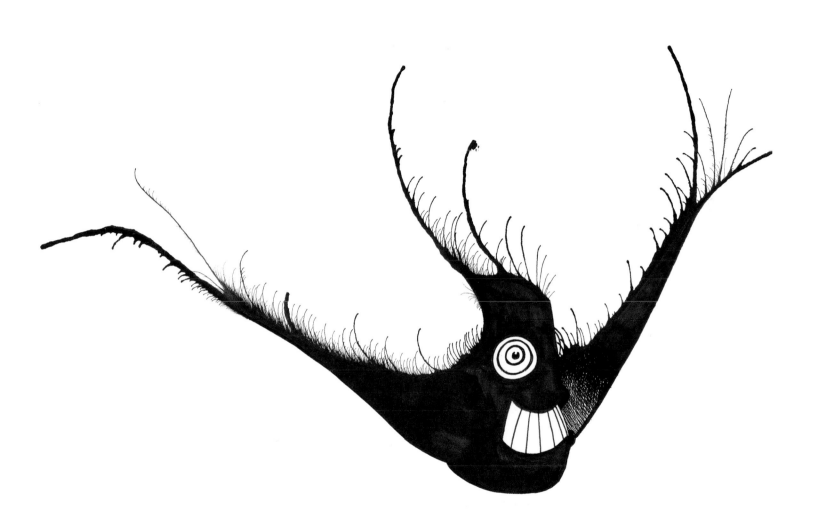

Pucci-meets-Alexander-McQueen-meets-Stella-McCartney-does-Adidas dog.
(They might deny it. We know differently!)

By Yi Shun Lai | February 04, 2007 at 12:58 P.M.

79

frogopteryx *(n)*
frog·op·ter·yx (fräg-äp-ter-iks)

Function: noun
Etymology: Middle English frogge, from Old English frogga + Greek pteryx wing;
akin to Greek pteron wing—more at FEATHER: a primitive crow-sized amphibian
of the early interia period of northern New Jersey having bestial characteristics
(as tentacle-like appendages and a long yellow ochre tongue). Known for its fondness
for Reddi-Wip and Chilean sea bass. Use caution when approaching.

By Capt. Robert Emmet Coogan, USMC | February 04, 2007 at 08:19 P.M.

Drawing:
Wednesday, 31 Jan 2007, 01:40 A.M.
Drawing posted:
Sunday, 04 Feb 2007, 01:11 A.M.

Tobias had been fishing for the last six hours. With absolutely no luck. He had heard nothing but good things about his particular patch of the great lake. Calmer waters. Decent-sized catches. Not very populated. It's not that nobody really knew about this part of the lake, just that they never seemed to come to this portion to actually fish. Tobias really didn't want anyone around anyway, if he could help it. The peace and quiet were what he looked forward to when fishing. He was getting plenty of the quiet. Not one nibble. He wasn't sure if it was the bait he used or maybe he was just having a bad day. The season called for more fish in the area, so he had extra bait in the water.

After no success, he decided to float up along the bank some. Tobias picked his new location and was ready to try for another go. He'd give it about an hour more. As he was sitting, motionless, his finger brushed up against a passing log. The interaction resulted in a rather large splinter, making Tobias give out a little yelp. He pulled out the splinter and dipped his finger in the water to soothe the bleeding wound. Definitely not the best day for Tobias.

Almost immediately, however, he finally got a bite. On the wounded finger. The sharp nip gave Tobias a start, which made him bring up all his tendrils, with their little thread-like fingers, out of the water. Curious, he dipped the bleeding appendage back into the water. Sure enough, a nibble once more. He toyed with the fish and then tensed the muscles and cartilage to morph the bitten portion into a rigid, hook-shaped barb. He opened his mouth wide, exposing his mossy tongue, and tossed the fresh catch straight into his mouth. Now armed with the knowledge of the proper bait, Tobias proceeded to fish with much better luck; albeit with bloody-fingered tentacles.

By Terry Tolleson | February 04, 2007 at 11:50 P.M.

Hungover second-story man, three-legged
peeping Tom on a bad hair day?
No… it's the robo-date for super models,
adjustable to any height.

By Annie Nordmark | February 05, 2007 at 08:26 A.M.

Grandpa Theobold never could get used to his prAna Protractor™ slacks.
Growing ever taller, Pappy Theo grumbled obscenities under his foul
eighty-four-year-old breath. "*@%&in' pants!" He'd cry from atop the ceiling.
We gave 'em to the old bugger so he could reach things on tall shelves,
but he claims it was easier before the pants. 344 dollars down the drain I guess.

By Sam Berkes | February 05, 2007 at 04:47 P.M.

Drawing:
Wednesday, 31 Jan 2007, 04:15 A.M.
Drawing posted:
Sunday, 05 Feb 2007, 04:55 A.M.

"I've got three reasons not to like you, Leon!"

Mr. Fim growled at Leon. His hair bristled with contempt for the rather new worker
to the group. Leon simply stared at Mr. Fim with a grim look on his face. "First of all,
your hair is all over the place. It's disgusting. People are complaining." Leon gave
a quizzical look at Mr. Fim. "Your clothes are also rather disgraceful. Multicolored pants
have a place in society." Again, Leon could only return what some might refer to
as "the confused German shepherd look." "Lastly, we're concerned about your height."
This was too much for Leon. What the hell did that mean? So what? What difference
did his height make in his line of work? His rage was only contained by his clenched teeth.

Here Leon was, listening to this blowhard go on about his hair, his clothes and his stature.
Yet, before him stood a tiki-faced man with what could only be described as ridiculous
bird feathers jutting out of his head. Pants that were two or three colors *and* striped. Worse yet,
Mr. Fim was shorter than him. Leon opened his mouth to let loose a volley of insults
when all of a sudden, Mr. Fim rose over three times his own height. His teeth gnashed back
and forth in his mouth and his eyes squinted down on Leon.

Leon apologized, made the requisite statement of "I'll work on it," and trudged back to
his office in his finely pressed khakis. What could he do? He couldn't quit. He was
the minority in this alien world of squatty, tiki-figurines that could apparently elevate
themselves much taller than a 6'2" human.

By Terry Tolleson | February 05, 2007 at 10:49 P.M.

170

Speed dating was always easy for Marc.
Until he got up from the table.
And until the second date.
And until the appetizers arrived at the table.

By Yi Shun Lai | February 06, 2007 at 06:57 A.M.

Drawing:
Wednesday, 31 Jan 2007, 04:30 A.M.
Drawing posted:
Tuesday, 06 Feb 2007, 04:00 A.M.

The *Muscidae Absaugung* (fly extractor) is often used in offset printing facilities. Instances of fly-shaped hickeys appearing on print blankets are reduced by nearly 100 percent after *Muscidae Absaugung* units are installed.

For a free 344-day trial, call 888-FLY-NO-MO.

That's nearly an entire year of fly-free printing! If you aren't completely pleased with your *Absaugung,* return it before the free trial period has expired and pay zilch! If satisfied, do nothing. Your credit card will be billed for the full amount.

Try one today, you won't be disappointed!

By Sam Berkes | February 06, 2007 at 08:11 P.M.

Tina was a terrific dancer, just look at her feet!
However, Ike said, "It was that tongue that threw me, man."

By Owen W. Swain | February 07, 2007 at 09:53 A.M.

Drawing:
Monday, 05 Feb 2007, 03:05 A.M.
Drawing posted:
Wednesday, 07 Feb 2007, 06:00 A.M.

The circular blade pierced through the soft edge and rolled straight across the entire length available. Red covered the silvery surface and seemed to clutch to it rather than slide off with ease. It was stainless steel, but it was heavily stained now. No denying the visceral slicing it left in its wake.

Kasuchev knew what he was doing. His actions [were] almost medical in their execution. One. Two. Three. Four. The slicing was without pause or remorse as the red adhered to the blade and oozed out over the yellow-white, protective covering. Chunks of sticky meat pushed about if they [weren't] immediately severed. It was sharp. Far sharper than it likely should have been, but Kasuchev was methodical with his instruments. With their use and their upkeep. His hair stood high; excited with every stroke. Every stroke that produced the color he so loved to see. He kept a rhythm by tapping his back foot as he sang a little cackle of a song to accompany every deep slice. He moved in front of an especially thick subject for his blade, not even bothering to clean his tool before piercing it swiftly. A long glide along the center.

Kasuchev stood in front of the long line of sliced pieces before him. Each one a work of art to him. He took pride in everything he saw in that row. All lined up perfectly, one next to another. All precisely sliced according to some measurement he held tight in his little brain. He would not be scorned or ridiculed or chastised for the insides spilling out over the shielding layer. Kasuchev was good at what he did, and he knew it. Even if none of his customers did. They just wanted their pizzas. His favorites had the most sauce.

By Terry Tolleson | February 07, 2007 at 09:27 P.M.

"I demand another quad latte, extra sprinkles on top!

I am the customer and the customer is always right—
I've not had too much coffee, man, and if you do not back away
from the coffee vault I am prepared to take extreme cutting
measures to breach the hull! Now get steaming or get stepping!"

By Victoria Koldewyn | February 07, 2007 at 11:10 P.M.

Monster 83 is named Seymour, not to be confused with the J.D. Salinger character. He's a flasher. But he only flashes fire hydrants. He's happy because there were three fire hydrants in the past two blocks.

By Catherine Matthew | February 08, 2007 at 08:41 A.M.

Hmm... maybe it's not happy... maybe... maybe it was so happy two days ago, and his mouth muscles went stiff in his smile, and now his family (a wife and 5,439 kids) got killed by a cranky and rebellious little meteor that did not like his wife's perfume, and he can't do anything but smile! Oh what agony :|

By Zivko Kondić | February 08, 2007 at 08:43 A.M.

The happy monster is happy on many counts, a few of them as follows:

HOORAY! Grape popsicles!!

HUZZAH! They didn't cancel *Dead Like Me* after only two seasons, after all!

SHAZAAM! I'm looking 4/4 and swingin' 7/4, hand me my sax, be cool my babies (relative of Conan O'Brien).

He's definitely on the Wang Chung Tonight Party Wagon.

Gimme a hoist up!

By Victoria Koldewyn | February 08, 2007 at 10:47 P.M.

When Jonas saw the ferry drift into the bay, he felt his day picking back up. Here he thought he missed it, but as it turned out he was early. He bobbed his head and shook his tail in rhythm with the piped-in music on the departures platform. His favorite song was playing. Yup. This was shaping up to be a good day. A fantastic free breakfast at Chez Dulche (he was the one-millionth customer), getting out of a speeding ticket (the officer was called away to a more pressing situation) and now he was early for the Histon Ferry. Jonas felt like he never had a mediocre day, let alone a good one. This was clearly a good day.

Michael looked down on Jonas from some distance. He remarked to Edward, who floated alongside him, "Wow—giving him a really good last day, eh?" Edward's only reply, with a half-hearted smile, "Everyone deserves an exceptional day at least once in their lifetime. Better late than never."

By Terry Tolleson | February 08, 2007 at 10:57 P.M.

84

Drawing:
Monday, 05 Feb 2007, 03:30 A.M.
Drawing posted:
Friday, 09 Feb 2007, 02:22 A.M.

Here you see the inimitable norf, in its home habitat of the sea of Mars. Scientists currently think that the sea is frozen, but they will soon find that it only appears to be frozen; it is actually a frothy mix of salt water, nitrogen and Dippin' Dots. In this nurturing environment, the inimitable norf raises her young, soaring through the slightly viscous mixture and keeping a close eye on her calf.

By Catherine Matthew | February 09, 2007 at 07:26 A.M.

Emlyn, age 4, says: These monsters are happy, sad and mad. They're going to Texas. They will live there. They will live outside. They will play with lots and lots and lots of toys. Their names are "Scary" and "Little."

By Sarah Schopp | February 09, 2007 at 11:18 A.M.

Englebrectt was born a large baby and never stopped growing. By the time he was three he was ten times the size of his father, who had to float around him to keep him in line. Englebrectt was a smart kid and became the protector of his village in the lawn. Whenever one hears a chunk in the lawn mower, that is Englebrectt, putting a kibosh on the chopping of the blades of grass.

By Thibaut Paciello | February 09, 2007 at 06:23 P.M.

The two swam with each other for the majority of the day. The smaller one was ready for her next step in life. The small growth spurt would be the first of many, but luckily, they weren't painful in any way. Mostly, the growing seasons saw several younglings very active and excited. The mothers would have quite the handful keeping up with their offspring's heightened energy levels. Ultimately, the biggest problem facing the parents of these little tykes (and by little, it [must be said that they] were the size of a small aircraft carrier) was their enormous appetites. Feeding these little guys was always an incredible undertaking. Good thing there are a lot of tasty meat sticks atop floating chunks of metal on the water's surface.

By Terry Tolleson | February 09, 2007 at 09:16 P.M.

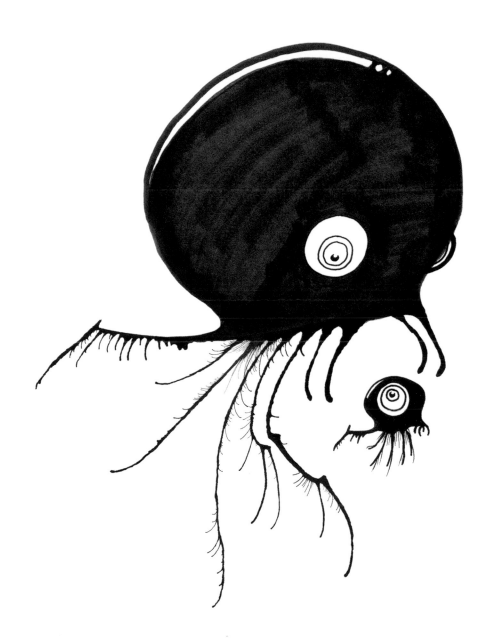

After more than a thousand years of vegetating in a cave beneath the ruins of Camelot, Sir Gawain finally purchased the tank-style armor-of-the-day wheelchair from the Merlin's magical lab winter sale and started the search for the Holy Grail again. Therefore he had to spit out the little black knight, who had slept in Gawain's throat for 947 years, 6 months, 2 weeks, 4 days and 21 hours.

By Björn Grau | February 10, 2007 at 05:02 A.M.

Feeling the full weight of the responsibility of only fourteen more Monsters to follow him, Philbert sends out his spawn in search of reinforcements.

By Owen W. Swain | February 10, 2007 at 05:08 A.M.

Johnny Weltlich hated taking the Botbus.

Public transportation really took a dive after Malcolm Bricklin was elected principal engineer of the Botbus program. Bricky must've been sippin' on some good tea, and I don't mean Lipton, to come up with this one. It spits you out when you get to your stop? Come on, seriously? Well, at least it doesn't blow up when rear-ended. But I wouldn't want to be sitting in one if that ever happened. You never know.

By Sam Berkes | February 10, 2007 at 09:52 P.M.

Drawing:
Monday, 05 Feb 2007, 03:45 A.M.
Drawing posted:
Saturday, 10 Feb 2007, 02:52 A.M.

86

In spite of her less-than-studied cat-walking skills, Beatrice quickly became the envy of West Coast supermodels.

In a private interview, she said her secret was in the pants—and it must be true, as close friends reported, "God knows, it isn't in her voice."

By Owen W. Swain | February 11, 2007 at 09:04 A.M.

Drawing:
Monday, 05 Feb 2007, 03:55 A.M.
Drawing posted:
Sunday, 11 Feb 2007, 04:01 A.M.

Here we see Hildegarde flaunting her pumps. Mmm hmm. That's just lovely, dear. Very flattering! And her dapper pinstripes are prêt-à-porter Vivants, a trés popular clothing line for women monsters who… love pinstripes… oh, your pardon I do beg, this is actually Gerald, who wears pumps with panache and wears a rhinestone belt made bespoke by VaVoom.

By Victoria Koldewyn | February 12, 2007 at 12:05 A.M.

You'd be grumpy too if your head was a giant bell!

The ceaseless noise! The sleepless nights! The tension headaches! At one point he tried to stop the awful ringing by muffling it with his hand... now, not only is his head as loud as ever, but his hand is flattened beyond repair... Now there is nothing for 87 to do but yell at the small children when they run too close and cause his head to start ringing.

By Sabeyen Daila | February 12, 2007 at 12:59 P.M.

Drawing:
Monday, 05 Feb 2007, 04:10 A.M.
Drawing posted:
Monday, 12 Feb 2007, 01:22 A.M.

We've just caught Wembly out. He's been handling the cookies in the cookie jar again. He doesn't need to withdraw the cookies to get his fix; his superlatively extra long phalanges are where his taste buds are. He saves himself a ton of extra poundage on his already beefed-out frame by just tasting. But the other members of his household don't have the same taste bud studded digits, so the cookies they eat are... tasteless. Wembly! For shame!

By Victoria Koldewyn | February 12, 2007 at 09:27 P.M.

He just rang my bell! I was so hoping he had my address. Of course, I'm afraid to answer. If he just leaves the flower, it'll be a happy day for me.

By Annie Nordmark | February 13, 2007 at 07:57 A.M.

Drawing:
Sunday, 11 Feb 2007, 06:25 P.M.
Drawing posted:
Tuesday, 13 Feb 2007, 02:14 A.M.

Yes, you guessed it: The lollipop flower is a key which monsters use to travel from one universe to the next.

As every monster knows, the planes between universes are slanted, so what you are seeing here is a monster—scientifically known as Trileggius Grinippius (aka the Three-Legged Grinner)—just beginning his slide from the monster universe into the human realm. This particular Trileggius is named Wilbur, and his tail is wiggling with excitement because he is entering this universe to visit his girlfriend, who has already traveled here. She is also a Trileggius (her name is Angelica), and she has promised him some Monster Love.

By Juliet Williams | February 13, 2007 at 06:46 P.M.

Hey! That's the first time ever (I am pretty darn sure) that we've seen the monster (or at least part of the monster) being drawn upside down—from YOUR perspective! Usually when you draw it upside down we're looking at it right-side up.

So it's all right-side up with this dandy, and it's all relative, and he's on the go with his red-light candyflower. Which doubles as his monster translator. He's an ambassador from the Planet of Love. Which is also known as Mars. And males are from Mars, ya know... he's going to visit the monsters on Venus. Which are female, ya know. Hence the candyflower/translator. Smart fellow, he.

By Victoria Koldewyn | February 13, 2007 at 11:14 P.M.

89

With a small "ding," the elevator doors slid open onto the all-too-familiar sign: 89 — MONSTERCORP: ACCOUNTING. Morris stepped out and turned the corner into his cramped cubicle. Was today Wednesday or Thursday? He sat and swiveled around to face the desk, reaching out to switch on his computer. He stopped, arm still outstretched. Frozen. There, lying across his keyboard, was the most gorgeous flower he'd ever seen.

A wave of panic washed over him. He looked around guiltily, convinced for one moment that he was in the wrong cubicle—but no, no, this was the right place. Those were his Post-its on the monitor, his pencils in the cup. That was his keyboard. Which meant that it was, presumably, his flower. Still hesitant, his mind blank, Morris reached out and grasped the stem. There was a small note attached. "Will You," it read, simply, "Be My Valentine?"

The more he looked at it, the more he had to accept that yes, it really was real. He had no idea what kind of flower it was; he'd never had much interest in such things... And it gently dawned on him that he'd never wanted anything more than how much he wanted, right this instant, to know the name of this flower. Who could it have been?

Morris got up and poked his head up over the top edge of his cubicle dividers. He felt himself smiling—just a little one at first, but soon a toothy grin that spread out across his whole face. His tendrils began waving, slowly, gleefully. For the first time since he'd started wearing it, his mood tie turned from its usual dull brown to white— bright white, speckled with pink polka dots.

Grinning like a maniac, and with all four of his hearts thudding, Morris looked out across the sea of cubicles. "Who," he whispered to himself, happy, all the morning's small woes forgotten, "could it have been?"

By Maya West | February 14, 2007 at 06:45 A.M.
Read the expanded version of this story on the DVD

I get the goose pimples when he waves his crown-hairs like that.

And he brought me my favorite: taffy-flower! Ever the gent, he's already softened it up for me. What a guy. I'd be his Valentine any day of the year. Especially if his taste in ties persists. And even more especially if he makes those ties from the tongue of the spotted Elderberry Blarfoog (the Blarfoogs of this species are regenerative folk, no worries—in fact, they need regular tongue-pulling to keep the gene pool varied).

By Victoria Koldewyn | February 14, 2007 at 10:39 P.M.

90

Drawing:
Sunday, 11 Feb 2007, 07:05 P.M.
Drawing posted:
Thursday, 15 Feb 2007, 06:00 A.M.

All the Valentine's Day chocolates and candies gave poor Lyle a bad case of gas. However, being a scientific creation of the great Dr. Humburt, Lyle was, unfortunately, created without an ejection point for all the gas to escape, such as most animals have on Earth. So now, instead of displaying loud and fruity bad manners for all of February 15, Lyle impressed his girlfriend with his newfound ability to fly, like a hot-air balloon.

Running with the idea, he opened a stall at the park. Attaching a laundry basket to his feet with fifteen-feet pieces of rope, Lyle was able to lift pet rodents and very small children into the air, for the small fee of twenty-eight dollars every fifteen minutes.

By Sabeyen Daila | February 15, 2007 at 05:06 P.M.
Read the expanded version of this story on the DVD

This is Fred the Turtleneck Monster.

He loves turtlenecks, and he wants to turn every shirt into a turtleneck. He is equipped with three independently blinking eyes—the better to spot turtleneck wannabes—and the ability to float and hover as he scopes out likely candidates. He is harmless and generally affable. He is easily distracted from his turtleneck quest by the offer of a bite of apple pie, stereograms and the color azure. Which means he is currently distracted by his own shirt.

By Juliet Williams | February 15, 2007 at 09:20 P.M.

It was no use. No matter how many times they tried to trip Erik, he would simply float up into the air. Even if they managed to clip him while he was completely unaware, his reflexes were almost catlike, and he could recover before completely falling. The most you would get from the attempt would be a blinking of his eyes as he hovered in midair, confused. Ultimately, several would try for no other reason than to see Erik cruise down the hallway on a cushion of air like some invisible, moving sidewalk. It served as good entertainment. And as long as Erik's long wisps of hair weren't being dunked in toilet water, he really didn't mind giving a float from one class to the next.

By Terry Tolleson | February 15, 2007 at 10:44 P.M.

91

Bicycle pump meets mullet meets monster.

By Jen Rodis | February 16, 2007 at 08:07 A.M.

Drawing:
Sunday, 11 Feb 2007, 07:45 P.M.
Drawing posted:
Friday, 16 Feb 2007, 02:42 A.M.

Rufus Arvind's been growin' that sweet rat-tail since who knows when. Poor guy's dumber than a box of rocks but he's got a great party trick up his sleeve. He limps (on account of a bear trap incident a few PBR's back) slowly up to a group of carousers and starts by flingin' that greased-up tail uh his back n' forth. Pretty soon his bulb of a nose'll start to grow. Like friggin' Pinocchio or sompthin. Seen him leave with some mighty fine tail usin' that one.

by Sam D. Berkes | February 16, 2007 at 08:19 P.M.

Ever since Reggie was just a little blob, he had always had this one cowlick in the back of his head that his mother couldn't get rid of. Reggie liked it though. He thought it made him look cool, like having a ponytail. No matter what she did though, and believe me she'd tried everything, it just wouldn't comb down or over or even up.

IT WAS JUST... THERE.

Finally at her wit's end one day, she tried cutting it off. Reggie's nose caved in. So rather than have her son look like he'd taken a cannonball in the face, she gave up and let him wear it long.

Over the years, Reggie became the life at parties having learned to manipulate his cowlick. He didn't like cherries, much less the stems, and couldn't wiggle ears he didn't have, so it was all he could do to impress the ladies.

In fact, it was at one of these parties that he met his now wife, a plastic surgeon with a nose fetish from Dubuque, Iowa.

by Ana Maria Seaton, Renmeleon | February 22, 2007 at 10:05 P.M.

92

Clive was alive / to the jive. After five / he thrived.

By Owen W. Swain | February 17, 2007 at 12:47 P.M.

Drawing:
Sunday, 11 Feb 2007, 07:50 P.M.
Drawing posted:
Saturday, 17 Feb 2007, 01:39 A.M.

Good day. I am Raoul, the famous footwear model. Today I am modeling the famous Blue Suede Shoes. Do I not look carefree and happy?
It is all in the walk! Watch!

By Heather Sebastian | February 17, 2007 at 01:26 P.M.

"Keep it real, my brotha, and the surreal will be your treat."

The words slid out his mouth
like a one-two in the bout.
One cool cat, so icy slick
D. Rovisi got penguins sick.
He carried the cool all the way
down to his shoes, blue suede.
Hands be trailin', all who knew
his struttin' walk, down East Avenue.

At the top of the game
Nowhere near
The bottom of the chain
No man to fear
Havin' all the fame
Gettin' all the cheer
Hookin' ev'ry dame
Awe from ev'ry peer.

D. Rovisi.
Delicious to many.
Every word he spoke,
Like honey from the Pope.
You should see his slide,
to his ride,
all his pride,
on the south side,
nowhere to hide,
respect is bona fide,
everything he's tried,
no one as guide,
no time to bide,
hella crib reside.

At the top of the game
Nowhere near
The bottom of the chain
No man to fear
Havin' all the fame
Gettin' all the cheer
Hookin' ev'ry dame
Awe from ev'ry peer.

By Terry Tolleson | February 17, 2007 at 11:01 P.M.

93

Drawing:
Sunday, 11 Feb 2007, 08:20 P.M.
Drawing posted:
Sunday, 18 Feb 2007, 03:20 A.M.

For months the photographer had waited across the street in a parked Fiat with tinted windows. HoHos wrappers and empty Slurpee cups littered the passenger seat. All the other paparazzi laughed at him—"Stick to the red carpets and charity auctions," they told him, "You'll never get a good shot of her like that." But he was a watcher, a quiet lurker so unlike the glittering young things he helped to foist upon the front pages. And perhaps it was this very difference that allowed him to see things a bit clearer, to begin to notice a thing or two about celebrity that the others missed.

He saw the attention swirl around a starlet like a smoke, for example, and if she took it for granted, he watched it harden into an invisible casing of narcissism she carried everywhere like a handbag. Soon, he knew, she'd forget to be kind to those without the smoke. She'd spend more and more time thinking about shoes and abs. She'd stop reading interesting books. And it would no longer occur to her to stop in a small boring town to have a beer inside an old tavern.

The photographer knew that if he waited long enough, that one night, emboldened by a false sense of innate beauty, the starlet would forgo the usual time-consuming beauty regime—the push-up bra, the girdle, the make-up—and would pop down to the corner twenty-four-hour health-food store for a bit of tahini she simply HAD to have on her quinoa. After all, who would possibly see her at this hour?

By Emily Reed | February 18, 2007 at 03:47 P.M.

Even though Haruko has been out of the clink (codeword for "pachinko") for a decade or so, he still succumbs to fits of spasmodic bumping about—which are actually quite comforting to him, since he spent more than two-thirds of his life in the pachinko. Every pachinko ball houses a small monster, you know, and the rumors of Yakuza brotherhood are probably specious.

By Victoria Koldewyn | February 18, 2007 at 08:53 P.M.

He is a teenage-geek-monster

that just asked a popular girl if she wanted to go and watch a film with him. (Something that you absolutely can call social suicide.) To his surprise, she says yes and gives him a kiss. So now he is in shock and he is actually walking on clouds.

By Ane Emilie Vold Mikkelsen | February 20, 2007 at 03:32 A.M.

Drawing:
Sunday, 11 Feb 2007, 08:40 P.M.
Drawing posted:
Monday, 19 Feb 2007, 01:00 A.M.

Well look at who we have here. It's Citrus, monster 92's mount! Citrus and 92 had a recent falling out when 92 got a new pair of shoes and cared to walk a couple places. As you can see, Citrus has wandered off into the badlands feeling neglected and has almost become a sort of vagabond. When Cit walks, he almost looks like he is floating. All of his appendages make him appear he is slithering across the floor, but he can get up to very fast paces—30 to 40 mph. Each of his mouth appendages are not normally that long, but 92 has not trimmed them since he got his shoes. Clementine likes them long, however, because he feels more in touch with his wild-man side. Each appendage hovers below a mouth giving Citrus a whole lot of mouths. He has two daughters and a son named Tangerine, Orange and Clementine respectively.

By David Conrey | February 19, 2007 at 05:42 A.M.

What's all the excitement surrounding Monster 94? Why does he accumulate throngs of onlookers and herds of paparazzi wherever he goes? Is he a prophet with news of the Apocalypse? Maybe he's discovered a way to fuel automobiles using only grass clippings? What if he's here to eat New York! Sadly, it is nothing as important as that. Monster 94 is just the Cruise family's new pet, Sweetums.

By Heather Sebastian | February 19, 2007 at 07:08 A.M.

Jerry was caught in a dilemma:

Do I eat my snacks or let them worship me a bit longer?

By Owen W. Swain | February 19, 2007 at 08:47 A.M.

Every year people travel from long distances to a tiny spot in the desert to greet the Snarkle monster. The Snarkle is a magical creature who blesses those he touches. He has to be careful about who he chooses, because his blessing and touch grants each person one wish of their choosing. This wish may be ANYTHING they want. From curing disease to a brand new Porsche. When he is ready to bestow his special gift, he picks three lucky people, rears back on his hind legs and shakes his head while mumbling the words that will make their wishes come true.

By Stacy Rausch | February 21, 2007 at 09:54 A.M.

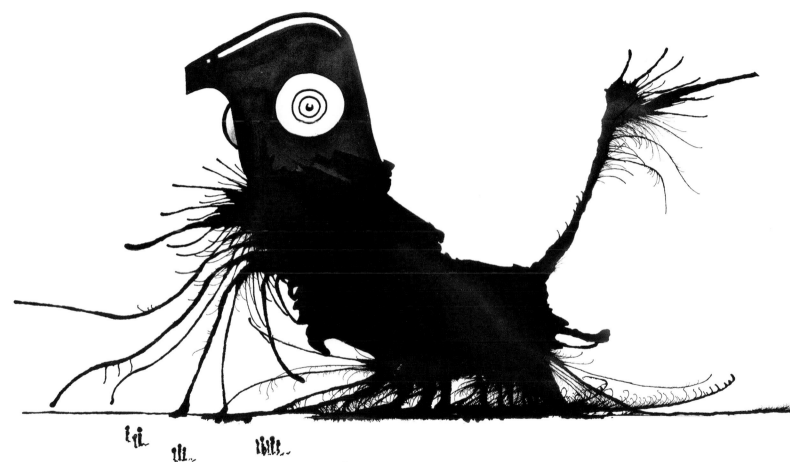

You there! What are you looking at??!

What's the matter with you, never seen a bearded monster before? Eh? EH? Well don't just stand there gawping, like a loose-jawed mackerel, go get me something to eat. Maybe a big bowl of caterpillars for ol' 95 eh? But don't go getting any of those fuzzy ones. The fur sticks in my teeth.

By Heather Sebastian | February 20, 2007 at 11:08 A.M.

Lester loved a lot of things. He loved his toothbrush, his radio, his fancy red shoes. But he loved nothing more than hopscotch. Everyone always thought it was so strange that a monster of his size would love such a childish game. Lester didn't care, though. Some mornings he would get up before dawn so that he could have two cups of coffee and a few practice hops before work. Then on his lunch break he would run around to the back of the building and have a few practice hops back there. He'd hop to the bus stop and he'd hop onto the bus. He'd hop at the grocery store and the post office. He'd hop all the time, just to make sure he could still hop.

Having so many feet sometimes became a huge problem, especially when he was tired. Sometimes feet numbers five and six would just stop wanting to hop. He took lots of vitamins and soaked his feet regularly to keep them happy. Last I heard, he was entering the National Hopscotch Championship in Roseburg. Everybody cheer for Lester!

By Stephanie Knauss | February 20, 2007 at 10:21 P.M.
Read the expanded version of this story on the DVD

Herman knew he had a problem, a serious one, but he couldn't pass up the chance to get another pair. Payless was having a sale. It didn't matter if he had thirty pairs in red already, these were "special." He stood at the window, salivating, hardly able to remain calm, his feet already dancing.

The fluorescent lighting inside glowed too bright, Herm could almost hear the slide of the bolt. Rushing past the salesmen he leapt the last few feet to victory and, shoes in hand, celebrated another day of conquest and, sadly, of addiction.

By Ana Maria Seaton, Renmeleon | February 22, 2007 at 09:02 P.M.

Drawing:
Sunday, 11 Feb 2007, 09:00 P.M.
Drawing posted:
Tuesday, 20 Feb 2007, 04:02 A.M.

96

Drawing:
Sunday, 11 Feb 2007, 09:15 P.M.
Drawing posted:
Wednesday, 21 Feb 2007, 03:40 A.M.

Of course Monster 96 is sour. She is the master of nineteen different languages—all of them now extinct. There's so much she wants to say... but no one, nowhere, can understand her. So she's taken a vow to speak only in riddles—but no one understands the riddles so she's in a diddle. Add the fact that she can no longer chew her food (monsters of her age often suffer from a sponging of the teeth—a liquid diet often being recommended) and I think her story is rather sad. I'd be grumpy too. And then you go and prod her with a disdainful finger. Outrageous. I think it's time people round here started showing Monster 96 some sympathy and respect. Think of her family.

By Paul Johnson | February 21, 2007 at 04:03 A.M.

It is a well-known fact that, until this very day, the Miss Universe contest has been rigged. But today changes all that! Celestine, of the beautiful planet 96, has become the first Miss Universe from anywhere but our little blue home planet. Of course, the Earth girls and their parents are plenty sore. In an exclusive clip we see the father of Miss Ireland actually poking poor Celestine, no doubt making obscene and rude remarks.

By Sabeyen Daila | February 21, 2007 at 12:09 P.M.
Read the expanded version of this story on the DVD

It's the newest *Spamalot* stage prop, the killer dragon.
He may look nice and a bit slow but he'll rip your face clear off.
If you doubt your courage or your strength, come no further.

-Bloody thing's not moving at all!-
(Cue animated finger to prod the beast)

AARRRRGGGGGHHHHHHH!!!!!!!

By Sam Berkes | February 21, 2007 at 08:14 P.M.
Read the expanded version of this story on the DVD

Monster 96 is the nicest monster. When he flies, his wings give all the people happiness. He sees that all poor people receive the food they need. He lives in a home and celebrates every holiday with the poor families. The reason he is so kind is because he is the last monster of his kind. There was a big fire where he lived and he was the only one that got out.

By Weston Tieler Rick, fifth grader | March 15, 2007 at 07:31 A.M.

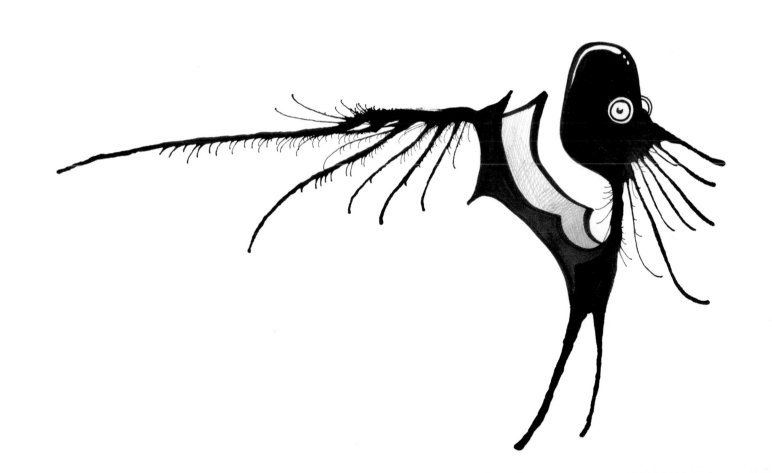

97

Drawing:
Wednesday, 21 Feb 2007, 10:55 P.M.
Drawing posted:
Thursday, 22 Feb 2007, 05:15 A.M.

One leg? Psh! That's what you think. Durek has twenty-seven, but is on the run from government officials for his development of invisibility. He's wearing invisibility pants with twenty-six leg holes, but you wouldn't know because his legs are now, obviously, invisible! His development would break all trust between countries and normal human interaction if it ever came into the wrong hands.

Fortunately for us, Durek really only uses his invisibility clothes to see movies for free and no one notices or cares (well, there was that one time someone tried to sit on him, but luckily for him, he slipped away quickly). Durek is also not that fat. To throw off his appearance, he took heed from his pet cockatoo and the hunchback from Notre Dame, putting on a hunchback suit and growing out his skull-skin. In this rendering of Durek, he is posing with his hand on his chin—a standard pose for someone who thinks as much as he does. If he didn't think that much, how could he have developed invisibility!?

By David Conrey | February 22, 2007 at 08:20 A.M.

Charles never considered having two eyes to be a handicap.

By Owen W. Swain | February 22, 2007 at 08:48 A.M.

HOW TO BE A GOOD MONSTER: Tips to stay wicked.

Step 1: Practice glaring. It is important to have a proper glare if one is to be menacing. One must also have various levels of said glare in order to get one's point across, without saying a word.

Step 2: Create an unusual hairstyle, preferably something that you have never seen on anyone else. We recommend going to the local daycare and having a five-year-old with scissors help you out.

Step 3: Obtain the proper outfit. It should say something of your personality and be unique. Don't use too many patterns or colors. 98 has chosen one key item, his shoes, to stand out.

Step 4: Perfect your evil laugh. Some go with an evil low laugh, some with a loud booming roar of a laugh. Some wickedly cackle. The choice is yours, but make sure it is perfectly honed.

Step 5: Get to scaring! Being with family or friends, test your techniques out and see what works and what doesn't. Technique is key in being an excellent monster.

Work hard! Play wicked! Be a MONSTER!

By Stephanie Knauss | February 23, 2007 at 03:14 P.M.
Read the expanded version of this story on the DVD

Drawing:
Sunday, 11 Feb 2007, 09:37 P.M.
Drawing posted:
Friday, 23 Feb 2007, 04:12 A.M.

The coolest monsters have terrible hygiene. In the monster equivalent of our human colleges, moldness is a trait similar to being completely ripped. As is evident by the dirty growth sprouting from the back of Monster #98's (Marcus's) head, he is one cool dude. This amount of dirtiness can only result in lots of itching. However, the scratching motion of Monster #98 is not an attempt to quell any itching. It's his signature dance move. Back in Monster College Marcus was known for keeping the dance floor alive. He only used one move... the back-scratch slide. Good thing it's an extraordinarily hip move!

By Logan E. Hasson | February 23, 2007 at 08:11 P.M.
Read the expanded version of this story on the DVD

Monster 98 has a happy life. She works in a bank (where she has recently been appointed to deputy manager, despite a small concern on her file about nibbling on the bullion—but that was years ago), she's got a great apartment just outside the city, and have you seen her new shoes? We see her here on her way home from work. As she left, Dennis (the cute one from marketing) flirted with her and asked her out for a drink, and when she got into the elevator she couldn't help leaning back against the mirror and giggling like a teenager. Let's wish her a good night...

By James Aylett | February 24, 2007 at 01:20 A.M.

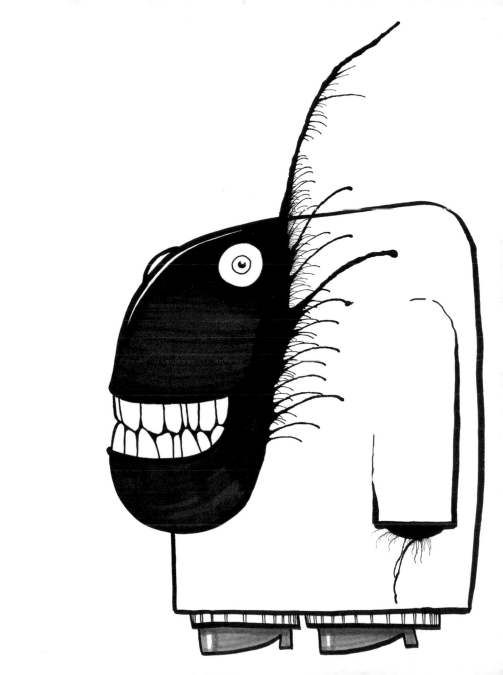

You are a professor and you bank on brains. You are a circuit breaker. You are the conduit. You are the nerve and the synapse. You are the truth and the light.

Close your mouth.

The university is the collage of your scrapbook; pension plan students. 401 equations. You are the residue and the substance, you are the resistance and the give, you are the redux and the text and the origination and the end and the repetition of the same and the same and the same.

Listen.

You know our names when we sign up for your class and you know us when we say something riveting and timeless. Otherwise, you forget us, or worse, you ignore us unless we somehow impress you with our desire for your knowledge. Subjectivity is out the window.

Sit still.

The professor listens with intent. We wonder how much she thinks about us after class. We wonder if the professor knows how much we give to her. We wonder and we wonder and the professor goes home and listens to the news and watches TV and reads through the next draft of her forthcoming novel. We walk to class and drive to class and think fully of the project we wept over, wrote and rewrote and gave up on. The professor arrives late with a latte in her hand. She strokes the sides of the cup as we argue our perspectives.

Work hard.

You think about the future of us. You are nothing without us and your jaw chews the food we provide you. You cannot sleep or eat without our synapses, our circuits, our repetitions, our intrigue, our desire. You are nothing without us; you are a homeless monster, a consumer, a Republican. You are a politician and an endangered animal. You are the truth and the light. I was a good student. Until I went to school.

By Brooke Nelson | February 24, 2007 at 08:50 A.M.

Ladies and gentlemen,
welcome to the Comedy Cave.

Our first comedian is so funny, he'll kill you. So please laugh anyway, cause if you don't, he's gonna kill you anyway. Please put your hands together, if you can reach 'em, for Mr. Henny Moungster.

Thank you. Thank you. Let's hear it for Frankie, our host. They just don't make 'em like him anymore. Let's thank the artist for that. Ha.

When I got to the airport this morning I told the ticket lady, "Send one of my bags to New York, send one to Los Angeles and send one to Miami." She said they couldn't do that. I told her, "Why not? You did it last week."

Thinking I'd get a few things redone I went to my doctor the other day and he told me I was crazy. I said, "Doc, I want a second opinion." He said, "Okay, you're ugly too."

I said, "Doc, why don't you come over to my place tomorrow for lunch?" He said fine. He was delicious.

Thank you, you've been a wonderful audience. Don't let me catch you following me home, or I'll have you over for breakfast.

By Bill Bibo Jr. | February 24, 2007 at 04:29 P.M.
Read the expanded version of this story on the DVD

Drawing:
Sunday, 11 Feb 2007, 10:40 P.M.
Drawing posted:
Saturday, 24 Feb 2007, 02:09 A.M.

100

Drawing:
Wednesday, 21 Feb 2007, 11:25 P.M.
Drawing posted:
Sunday, 25 Feb 2007, 07:22 A.M.

Original Viola Coda by Logan Hasson

So often when we hear the word *monster*, we think of the dark ones; those that hide under the bed, or lurk in the shadows, or perhaps, those who creep into our ear at night to suck on our brain—the numbskullians. Or some other unsavory character who relishes in giving monsters a bad name. But not all monsters are like that. Monster 100 most certainly isn't. For this is Gavin.

Gavin had always followed his own path. And if that meant people laughed at him for wearing oversized knitwear, then that was just fine with him. After all, a laugh was a laugh and the world was a better place for hearing it.

He had a fear of the dentist, which some people thought irrational, but Gavin would just say "What's irrational about being scared of a masked man sticking sharp objects into your mouth?" And as always he had a point. He also had one of the lousiest music collection known to monster-dom—for I kid you not when I say it consisted of ELO, Kate Bush and Barry Manilow.

His gift was to leave you happier for meeting him.

But the cost of such a gift was to never find some-one to share his life with. Oh, he had girlfriends, had even married and had a beautiful daughter called Beatrice, but he'd lived his life without meeting his soul mate. Until last year when he met a beautiful female monster. The next few months were the happiest of Gavin's life, but they weren't to last. One day, out of the blue he was snatched away. Sometimes, when one monster is missing, the whole world seems empty.

By Simon Darwell-Taylor
February 25, 2007 at 12:42 P.M.
Read the expanded version of this story on the DVD

Ladies and gentlemen, it is a touching scene here at 344 as Elmer N'Chidway, the official Ambassador for all of Stefan G. Bucher's 100 Monsters, bids us a fond, sad but heartfelt farewell and is lovingly escorted from the scene by Mr. Bucher himself. But what's this? Ambassador N'Chidway has left behind an egg, a pod, a seed or some sort of off-spring. Could we be looking at the next generation of monsters? We have assembled a team of our most expert monsterologists to speculate:

Dr. Wilberforce Snodgrass (see Monster 55): Clearly this egg is that of the Canistentacula monster—a.k.a. Dogface with Tentacles. This monster will hatch in a mere six weeks and will require a steady diet of squid and chicken bones.

Dr. Hank Flapper, specialist in winged monsters: It's going to be a Pteradonster, a flying reptile monster with a long, skinny tongue that it uses to zap its prey from as high as twenty-five feet in the air.

Dr. Mildred Quince, monsterbotanologist: Heavens, it's not an egg, it is a spore from the very rare Mushroomibilius. This is a monster that lives deep in the Russian tundra. Though it never grows taller than six inches, it can achieve diameters of up to two miles. It reproduces by releasing spores just like this one, which are fertilized when they land in pools of water that contain human dandruff.

Dr. John Chin, supermonsterologist: I have studied this artifact at great length and the only conclusion that my data forces me to reach is that this is, in fact, Stefan G. Bucher's brain, in Sharpie form.

There you have it, ladies and gentlemen. The dispute will rage on in the monsterologist community about the exact identity of the item left behind by Ambassa-dor N'Chidway. Until next time, I am your ever-intrepid reporter, Howard Talksalot, signing off.

By Juliet Williams | February 25, 2007 at 12:49 P.M.
Read the expanded version of this story on the DVD

Bixby William, the lonely man, treats us to a lovely thumbs-up.
His pensive promulgation of our precious daily monster was par
for the course. He's left us a treat too, a giddy little monstegglet.
You see in his world, much the same as with seahorses,

the male is the one to hatch the young.

Good Bixby has given us a lovely cliffhanger ending to keep us
hungry for more monster goodness. I can't wait to see what's in store
for us next week.

By Sam Berkes | February 25, 2007 at 09:02 P.M.

Monsters, as we all know, are a very rare sight to behold. Their population,
while not yet small enough to be classified as "endangered," is on the
decline. The very rare glimpses that are afforded the lucky human are
few and far between, and the idea of encountering one every day is
extraordinarily far-fetched. Yet, somehow, the last few months have proved
miraculous, and we lucky few have seen one hundred of these rarities.
They are a sight to behold, indeed! While it has been fun to view monster
after monster, we all knew it would only be a matter of time before we
had seen them all. One hundred days later, and the fears of many have been
realized! There is, however, hope! The birth of a new monster brings with
it the promise of a grand future. The monster population as we now know
it will grow at a rate of one monster per week. How exciting this is!
While an era of daily monster sightings has come to a close, we humans
know that it won't be long before the next one makes an appearance.

We shall be waiting, little one.

By Logan E. Hasson | February 25, 2007 at 09:56 P.M.

The mother is so blessed to give her birth. She is following the trend
of her ancestors. She leaves her young. This is cyclical.

There is much dispute over the traditional manner in which the
mother leaves her young to hatch and then live on her own. They call
this species to arms. The species has only its history. The species is
a tradition and a tradition of traditions. We change with our language.

The species began as a transient group, wafting from one page to
another, flipping and giddy with life. Like the evolving game of
telephone, the message changes, the message changed, and the

species no longer supports its young. No need. Someone else
comes along and pokes the egg, prods it, learns it. Someone else
supports it. This is trust. This is communal. In the purest sense.
The community of the species forwards it and prods it and forces it
to become what it is. There is no definition, there need not be finality.
The species lives on with the help of the world.

It is born again and again in the palm of the sky.

By Brooke Nelson | February 26, 2007 at 11:49 A.M.

Breeding monsters had never been the career he'd envisioned for himself.
There had been a smooth path laid out for him in printing: His great-
granddad (the late Mr. Gutenberg) had invented the printing press, after all.
There was something good and solid about spreading "The Witches'
Hammer" across the European continent. Until the day fate chose to
cross his yellow brick road with inkblots.

Their biggest press (nicknamed "The Monster") had been spewing out
pages and pages of "The Witches' Hammer" for the French market when
the operator noticed big trouble: Almost every page was stained with
thick drops of ink that leaked across the page when he tried to brush them
off. The Monster was defective. While his workmen worked around the
clock to save the leaking press, Gutenberg's great-grandson took it upon
himself to search for pages that could be rescued. The less that had
to be reprinted, the better. They were working on a tight schedule here.

Deep into the night the printing press owner leafed through pages and
pages, looked at inkblot after inkblot. The owner realized he was ruined.
With watery eyes he sighed. If only his precious Monster hadn't
abandoned him... the only monster he had allowed to live in this world.

Before his tired eyes the blots on the pages started to shift and change.
They grew bigger, getting hands and feet. He shook his head in an attempt
to clear his view. The shaking only awakened the creatures, making them
hop from page to page.

Years later he found himself watching inkblots grow on paper, and
caressing newborn monsters. This one was his favorite. She'd given him
many eggs that hatched into monsters to admire, monsters that would
never make it into "The Witches' Hammer," and that would make their big
Monster-Mama proud.

By Frances Lievens | February 26, 2007 at 02:11 P.M.
Read the expanded version of this story on the DVD

This final monster
Leaves his world behind
In order to see what else lies
In the world outside.

By Ben Boatwright | February 26, 2007 at 04:10 P.M.

The spiritual heirs of John Nevil Maskelyne would no doubt take issue with the adjective "spiritual," but nevertheless, here they are: a group of magicians, experts, textperts, choking smokers and skeptics taking time off from their endless pursuit of rogue billet readers to meet in Conference Room A of a Holiday Inn in Fresno to puzzle out the existence of Monster 100. The more taxonomically inclined ask "Is Monster 100 a monotreme?"

The case for: He has hair and he just laid an egg.

The case against: Teeth.

The prevailing opinion, then, is that perhaps the egg-laying is just some clever legerdemain ("legerdederriere"?) on 100's part. He does bear a passing resemblance to Ricky Jay, or at least something Ricky Jay would be interested in (they say broadsheets begin to resemble their owners). Where is Ricky Jay, anyway? Shouldn't he be here? They put the video on a loop and they determine: There is some funny business going on with that second sheet of paper. Perhaps that's how it was done? But no one can pinpoint it exactly. Murmurs from the crowd: "Eggs are common enough magician props"; "Nothing up my sleeves"; "Regardless, man, you should have seen them kicking Edgar Allan Poe."

And then someone says, quietly: "The great mentalist, The Amazing Dunninger, once said there is one primary rule in the fakery of spirit mediumship" (one assumes that this extends to Magical Egg Apparition); he continues: "And that is, to concentrate upon persons who have suffered a bereavement." The speaker looks around the room: Everyone there is suffering a bereavement, for 100 is the last of the Daily Monsters. The magicians look around at each other for a moment and then shuffle sadly out of the conference room. They're in no state to crack this one, and anyway, Martin Gardner is going to do a PowerPoint about the time he had a fistfight with Uri Geller and they don't want to miss it.

As they file out, the video is still on a loop, and that Logan Hasson viola piece comes up again as the last magician is turning off the light. Listening to it, he can almost put some words to it: "I am the eggman. They are the eggmen. I am the walrus," but then as immediately as it starts to make sense, he has lost it again, and so he snaps the lights off at last. Goo goo g'joob g'goo goo g'joob.

By Patrick Mortensen | February 28, 2007 at 06:17 P.M.

It's not easy being last. I have always been last. But that's not as bad as being the one always being made fun of.

Ever since I can remember, I have been made fun of. Friends, if you can call them that, always made jokes about my rounded head and skinny nose. Heck, I never thought I was that different. And the shorty jokes too. Me short? I'm almost two feet tall!

It was assumed I would always be the last. But then it happened. I surprised them all the day 101 came. No one could believe it! No one had ever made a new one by themselves. But I did! And from now on there will be someone else that's last. Not me, not Mr. 100. And I hope 101 has lots of problems with it too. I hope 101 is short, stinky, curly nosed, square-headed and RED! Yeah, that's what I hope…

Well, unless he wants to be my friend.
Then I hope 101 is just as unique as me.

By John Asumendi | March 02, 2007 at 05:29 A.M.

THE FIRST TIME

A voice from nowhere speaks loudly, but with a gentle calmness. *"Where are you?"* A lone figure, sitting in a grassy field, looks about confused but not frightened. He scans his surroundings looking for the source of the voice. Eventually responding, unintimidated. *"In a field."* The dialogue begins.

What do you see? — Grass. — *What else do you see?* — A desk. — *Where is the desk?* — I'm sitting at it. — *Why are you sitting there?* — I was looking through a book. — *What book?* — I don't know. There's nothing in it. Just blank pages. — *There is nothing on the cover of the book?* — No. It, too, is blank. — *How long have you been looking at the book?* — I don't know. I don't know how long I have been here. Wherever "here" is. — *Close the book.* — OK.

THE SECOND TIME

The individual is standing in the field holding a book tight to his chest. A voice from nowhere begins a conversation.

Where are you? — Standing in the field. — *What are you doing?* — Looking at a book. — *What book?* — The one I am holding. — *What is the book about?* — Creatures. Beings. Monsters. — *What does it say about them?* — Nothing. It's just picture after picture of them. — *Did you draw them?* — Yes. Yes, I think I did. — *How?* — I thought about them. They appeared in my head and then on the pages. — *How many pages?* — A hundred. — *Close the book.* — OK.

THE THIRD TIME

A lone figure, carrying a small book, stands in a grassy field. Staring off into the horizon. Without warning, a low, steady voice announces from somewhere. It's the same question. *"Where are you?"*

"I'm in a field. A grassy field. The same field I have been in for days. Months, even. There is nothing new. Nothing different. Well... the desk is gone — but that's because I have since left the area it was in and do not know where I am now in relation to it. This field is enormous. Without end. There is nothing here but the grass, me and this book." He is clearly tired, but not necessarily angry. The voice replies, *"There is no one else there? Nothing else there?"* Confused, the man quickly responds, "No."

After a few silent moments, something appears on the horizon. Floating a few meters above where the grass meets the sky's never-ending reach. As the object comes closer, he can make out a familiar shape. A bird. Not just any ordinary bird. This bird is familiar to him. A realization dawns! He immediately flips open the book to the first page. There it is. The odd image stares back at him from the page whence he drew it. When it flies overhead, he can clearly see that it is, in fact, the very bird he created in the book. Its long, toucan-style, amber beak chattering sounds of delight as it struggles against the weight of its enormous shoes. The man is completely in awe at seeing such a thing floating in front of him. Thousands of questions begin to form in his mind. Before he has a chance to vocalize any of them, however, another shape appears on the landscape. And another. Soon the horizon is dotted with unknown specters and forms.

And one by one, they converge on the man in the grassy field. And one by one, they are identified by him from a page in the book. A walrus-looking beast sporting a shredded necktie to his left. On his right, a briefcase-toting Rollerblader next to a large, hairy-mouthed juggernaut. Over to the left, a single branch sprouted from the earth to provide a perch for a banana-beaked, spindly legged bird. Amongst the crowd of monsters approached another, walking directly toward him. A tiny frame ambling before him with a smile that showed jagged teeth and lipped with several whiskers. A thick turtleneck draped its body as it made its way to the man in the grassy field. He recognized this figure right away as the last one drawn in the book. An exact copy, down to the tiniest detail.

It stopped in front of him and gave a very pleased smile as it squatted down, the sweater hiding its feet. A little dance ensued and before long, it rose up and gave another happy grin with squinted eyes. Something was visible below it. The man extended his hand for the diminutive figure to hop onto his hand. When he slid his hand back, he could see a small egg sitting upright on the ground. He prodded the egg, but it only bounced excitedly. Returning his attention to the horde surrounding him, he asked out loud, "Where did they come from?"

The voice replied, *"Each one was asked the same question you were, 'Where are you?' and each one replied the same, 'In a dark place. Lonely and lost.' Within a day of asking the question, they answered the same as you the second time, 'In a grassy field.' Each day, for a hundred days, a new creature would come into being. Each day, for a hundred days, each one would answer the same both times asked. They came from you by printing them in that book."*

Stunned, the man gazed at the group and then back at the egg. He flipped through page after page and could not find anything remotely like it. All the other monsters were exact replicas of his illustrations, except this egg. This egg was new. This egg wasn't his.

What of the egg? — *The egg is the future.* — I didn't draw the future. — *No one can.* — What's inside? — *No one knows.* — I'm ready. — *Close the book.* — OK.

By Terry Tolleson | February 25, 2007 at 03:13 P.M.

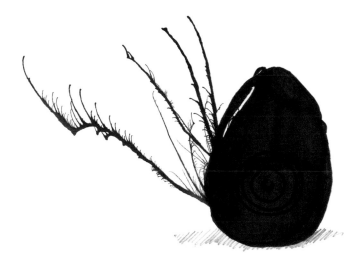

MONSTER FAMILIES

- 25% Scientists
- 20% Happy Monsters
- 18% Turf Monsters
- 15% Dramatic Monsters
- 15% Airborne Monsters
- 7% Surf Monsters

INTERESTING FACT: Some of the monsters are so bigger than the people. And yet, none of the biggest monsters is the ones that would make our planet. Jupiter look like an understated existence—not well read life. Just how without regard keeping places out of their severity overnight.

GLOBAL MONSTER DISTRIBUTION

0.06%	Unknown!
0.17%	Central America
0.27%	Africa
1.83%	Oceania
3.33%	South America
5.45%	Asia
32.84%	Europe
56.06%	North America

TOP 10 MONSTER AUTHORS

102 posts	Sam Berkes
82 posts	Victoria Koldewyn
75 posts	Terry Tolleson
35 posts	Alexander Pollard
32 posts	Yi Shun Lai
30 posts	Owen W. Swain
24 posts	Jessica L. Beers
24 posts	Ben Boatwright
23 posts	Juliet Williams
19 posts	Annie Nordmark

WHERE ARE PEOPLE WATCHING MONSTERS?

001. United States	078. Macedonia
002. Germany	079. Pakistan
003. Canada	080. Kazakhstan
004. United Kingdom	081. Nigeria
005. Spain	082. Malta
006. Japan	083. Bangladesh
007. France	084. Algeria
008. Norway	085. Mauritius
009. Brazil	086. Qatar
010. Australia	087. Andorra
011. Netherlands	088. Honduras
012. Mexico	089. Jamaica
013. Israel	090. Bosnia and Herzegovina
014. Hungary	091. Guam
015. Austria	092. Barbados
016. Italy	093. Paraguay
017. Belgium	094. U.S. Virgin Islands
018. Switzerland	095. Lebanon
019. Sweden	096. Brunei Darussalam
020. Greece	097. Bahamas
020. Argentina	098. Netherlands Antilles
021. Singapore	099. Martinique
022. Portugal	100. Kuwait
023. Denmark	101. Belarus
024. Chile	102. Bermuda
025. Finland	103. Cayman Islands
026. New Zealand	104. Moldova
027. Korea	105. Fiji
028. Poland	106. Macao
029. Ireland	107. Liechtenstein
030. Romania	108. Mongolia
031. South Africa	109. Anguilla
032. Turkey	110. Aruba
033. Russian Federation	111. Sri Lanka
034. Colombia	112. Nepal
035. India	113. Myanmar
036. Bulgaria	114. Saint Lucia
037. Slovenia	115. Nicaragua
038. Malaysia	116. Oman
039. Lithuania	117. Georgia
040. Philippines	118. Cambodia
041. Thailand	119. Yemen
042. Venezuela	120. Namibia
043. Hong Kong	121. Zaire
044. China	122. Belize
045. Taiwan	123. Bhutan
046. Czech Republic	124. Cote D'Ivoire
047. Peru	125. Libyan Arab Jamahiriya
048. Iceland	126. Botswana
049. Croatia	127. Antigua and Barbuda
050. Indonesia	128. Albania
051. Luxembourg	129. French Polynesia
052. Estonia	130. Laos
053. Latvia	131. Tanzania
054. Costa Rica	132. French Guiana
055. Slovakia	133. Palestinian Territory
056. Iran	134. Saint Vincent
057. Uruguay	and the Grenadines
058. United Arab Emirates	135. Kenya
059. Serbia and Montenegro	136. Armenia
060. Saudi Arabia	137. Senegal
061. Puerto Rico	138. Zambia
062. Ukraine	139. Suriname
063. Dominican Republic	140. Faroe Islands
064. Egypt	141. Turks and Caicos Islands
065. Vietnam	142. Guadeloupe
066. Jordan	143. Azerbaijan
067. Cyprus	144. Mozambique
068. Panama	145. Maldives
069. Guatemala	146. Ghana
070. Uganda	147. Afghanistan
071. Ecuador	148. New Caledonia
072. Morocco	149. Syrian Arab Republic
073. Trinidad and Tobago	150. Cuba
074. Bolivia	151. Cameroon
075. Tunisia	152. British Virgin Islands
076. El Salvador	153. Sudan
077. Bahrain	154. Guyana

THE MONSTER AUTHORS INDEXED, ALPHABETIZED AND NEATLY STACKED, JUST FOR YOU

numbers indicate monster

Asumendi, John	100
Aylett, James	98
Barry, Laura	23
Beers, Jessica L.	54, 59, 61, 63–66, 68–70
Berkes, Sam	01–03, 05, 11–13, 17, 18, 20, 24, 28, 29
	32, 33, 36, 41, 45–47, 49–51, 54, 55, 62, 63
	65, 66, 68, 72, 75–77, 80, 81, 85, 91, 96, 100
Bibo Jr., Bill	49, 56, 69, 78, 99
Boatwright, Ben	35–37, 39, 40, 46, 48, 100
Bovone, Adriane	48
Britt, Kyle J.	42
Conrey, David	94, 97
Coogan, Robert E.	79
Cygnus	01
Daila, Sabeyen	64, 68–70, 76, 87, 90, 96
Darwell-Taylor, Simon	11, 19, 20–24, 100
Doria, Amanda	22
English, Scott	32, 41
Fedele, Amy	40, 60
Fletcher, Kyle	12
Gates, Emmo	74
Grau, Björn	85
Hasson, Logan E.	98, 100
Himes, Amber	17
Hunt, William	75
Johnson, Paul	96
Knauss, Stephanie	37, 38, 43, 95, 98
Koehler, Megan	1, 11
Koldewyn, Victoria	42, 50, 52, 57, 60, 61, 65, 68,
	72, 75, 82, 83, 86, 87–89, 93
Kondić, Zivko	83
Lai, Yi Shun	32–34, 37, 38, 44, 47, 49, 73, 75, 79, 81
Laporte, Sara	25
Latzke, Matt	66, 67, 70

Lee, Susan	4, 11, 25
Lievens, Frances	100
Madison, Jessica	54
Matthew, Catherine	83, 84
Mayes, Azalea	37
McTyre, Jake	60, 63
Metzner, Joerg	9, 12
Morley, Catherine	10, 17
Mortensen, Patrick	100
Murphy, Emily H.	18
Nelson, Brooke	13, 25, 27, 55, 70, 99, 100
Ngo, Danielle	15, 17, 73
Nordmark, Annie	51, 57, 78, 80, 88
Paciello, Thibaut	84
Pollard, Alexander	8, 24, 26, 28, 30, 31, 40, 53
Pringle, Pete	14
Quintin, Thaddeus	53
Rausch, Stacy	94
Reed, Emily	58, 92
Rick, Weston Tieler	96
Rodis, Jen	10, 91
Rodrigues, Jordan	26
Schopp, Sarah	22, 84
Scott, Thomas	33
Seaton, Ana Maria	91, 95
Sebastian, Heather	92, 94, 95
Swain, Owen W.	59, 60, 67, 73, 76, 81, 85, 86, 92, 94, 97
Tischler, Selma	41, 43
Tolleson, Terry	34–36, 39, 45, 50, 52, 57, 61
	71, 74, 77, 79, 80, 82–84, 90, 92, 100
Tomlinson, Pimpom	52, 53, 65
Townsend, Gareth	9
Vold Mikkelsen, Ane E.	93
West, Maya	89

Whitman, Katy	58, 60, 67, 73
Williams, Juliet	53, 59, 62, 64, 67, 72, 88, 90, 100
Witman, Diane	18
Wodinsky, Shoshana	27, 29, 44
Wray, Amanda	4
Zirkunow, Simon	16

MORE MONSTER AUTHORS
featured on the Monsters in Motion DVD

Hans Akrok, Tiago Allen, Jennifer Beaman, Jim Biancolo,
Rasmus Blaesbjerg, Linda Blakely, Dave Conrey,
Adriene Crimson, Russell Davies, Luc Debaisieux,
Jonas Forslund, Shane Guymon, Whitney Hadwin,
Lisa Hansen, Laura Haraké, Erik Kaiser, Ellie Katona,
Matheus Komar, Shelley Krause, Henning Krauspe,
Amy Lenzo, Nikki Leeper, Robert Leeper, Janet Mayes,
Keith McCord, Jose A.Mercado, Audrey L. Oguss,
Kelly Planer, Julia L. Ritchey, Laura Swayne, Baris Tansel,
Cynthia Teigland, Telvin, Evangeline Than, Missy Tolleson,
Nadiah Jemoni Tucker

CREDITS
Editor: Amy Schell | Acquisitions Editor: Megan Patrick
Art Director (HOW Books): Grace Ring
Book Design: Stefan G. Bucher, obviously
DVD Interface Design: Kenn Rudolph
DVD Production: Kenn Rudolph, Tim Moraitis
kennrudolph.com | moraitisdesign.com

THE MONSTER COLOR CODE ANOTHER SUBTLE WAY OF UNDERSTANDING YOUR MONSTER BOOK MORE FULLY

And come on... you know you want to. Anyone can pick up a book, flip through it, have a few cheap laughs and be done with it. But for a real bibliophile such as yourself, understanding the nuanced ballet of design and content is the key to letting blossom the full flower of aesthetic appreciation. You've grabbed your loupe to read this section. You're on the right path: Clearly, my love for you is not misplaced. (The color code was Grace Ring's idea, by the way.)

HAPPY MONSTERS
What can I say? These monsters are having a good time. Of course, they're enjoying themselves. If they have any doubts about their purpose in life, or what it all means, they're not letting it get them down. They're just ... happy. (Yeah... I don't really get it, either.)

DRAMATIC MONSTERS
There is something not right with these monsters. Either they're up to something, or some little thing set them off—making them angry, or sad, or maybe they're just hungry. Whatever it is, they're not happy, and they're not shy about letting you know. (Now this I can understand.)

SURF MONSTERS
These are creatures of the deep. To say they live underwater would be a gross oversimplification. Many of them swim in or float on a sea of molten metal, or in the hidden oceans under Europa's mantle of ice. These are monsters of the greatest mystery. (Most of them are nice guys, though!)

TURF MONSTERS
Turf Monsters roam the land. They're just as intelligent as the Happy and Dramatic Monsters. Many of them have better manners and could beat you at chess. What puts them in a different category is the fact that they don't wear pants. In the monster world that's a big deal.

AIRBORNE MONSTERS
Now, this is a very simple category: Airborne Monsters fly. Of course, they have very different ways of taking to the air. Some have wings, some are lighter than air, some will inflate their heads, and yet others will simply wrestle gravity to the ground with a cogent argument.

THE SCIENTISTS
If monsters were disciplined enough to establish an elected government, these guys should run it. The thing is, they'd never stand a chance in a general election. They're overqualified and undercool. They wear lab coats and make Star Trek references at the most inappropriate moments. (I love 'em!)

MEET YOUR MONSTER DVD:

Here is a quick directory of the fabulous goodies
you'll find on the *Monsters in Motion* DVD:

TOP DRAWER

The top drawer holds all 100 Daily Monster clips. You can watch them
individually, in sets of 20, or you can strap yourself in and absorb
all 100 monsters back to back to back. If you choose to go that route,
please know that I can't be responsible if you have a religious
experience or a seizure or both. Who knows what almost two hours
of sustained time-lapse Sharpie noises do to the human brain?

(I'm assuming that you're human. If you're not, please contact me. I need a ride home.)

BOTTOM DRAWER

01 ✏ REGULAR SPEED MONSTER
If you ever wanted to see me draw a monster in real time,
without any fancy time-lapse trickery, this is the clip for you.

02 ✏ OPEN SOURCE MONSTERS
Would you like to make some monsters of your own?
This link will lead you to a PDF with 10 Open Source Ink Blots
that let you get in on the fun!

03 ✏ A WORD FROM MR. BUCHER
Are you up to a few minutes of yours truly rambling on?
I couldn't resist the temptation of leaving you a little message.

04 ✏ THE COMPLETE MONSTER TEXT
This link gives you access to a PDF with the entire transcript
of the first 100 days of the Daily Monster blog, complete
with my daily intros, the unedited stories from this book,
and many extra tales that just wouldn't fit in these pages.

05 ✏ UPSTAIRS NEIGHBORS
Meet the original monsters that started it all
with this PDF teaser for *Upstairs Neighbors*.

THANK YOU:

This book wouldn't exist without all the amazing
people who came to the website and have become
a part of my little experiment. This has been one
of the most extraordinary experiences of my life,
and I can't thank you enough for making it so.
This book is for you.

Thank You to all the kind people who wrote about
the Daily Monsters on their sites, and spread the word.

Thank You to Megan Patrick at HOW Books who
took a chance and made this book happen. Thank You
to Amy Schell, my excellent editor, and to HOW
Books art director Grace Ring, who both helped me
shape the thing into the nifty item you're holding
in your hands today.

A big Thank You also goes to Kristin Ellison, the editor
of my first book, who taught me many things that
I wasn't ready to learn back in 2004, but that made
both that book and this one immeasurably better.

A very special Thank You to the indefatigable
Kenn Rudolph and Tim Moraitis, who spent many
long nights crafting the Monster DVD into
a little piece of art for you. Gentlemen, you rock!

Thank You to my excellent shrink, for obvious reasons.
Thank You always to my brilliant and patient friends,
who make me laugh and keep me sane. (Special
Thanks to Karla and Jen.) And of course, Thank You
to my mom and dad.

FINALLY:

Failure is never as frightening as regret.
Don't worry. It'll all work out.